Hands-On Markov Models with Python

Implement probabilistic models for learning complex data sequences using the Python ecosystem

Ankur Ankan
Abinash Panda

BIRMINGHAM - MUMBAI

Hands-On Markov Models with Python

Commissioning Editor: Sunith Shetty
Acquisition Editor: Varsha Shetty
Content Development Editor: Karan Thakkar
Technical Editor: Sagar Sawant
Copy Editor: Safis Editing
Project Coordinator: Nidhi Joshi
Proofreader: Safis Editing
Indexer: Aishwarya Gangawane
Graphics: Jisha Chirayil
Production Coordinator: Shraddha Falebhai

First published: September 2018

Production reference: 1250918

Published by Packt Publishing Ltd.
Livery Place
35 Livery Street
Birmingham
B3 2PB, UK.

ISBN 978-1-78862-544-9

www.packtpub.com

`mapt.io`

Mapt is an online digital library that gives you full access to over 5,000 books and videos, as well as industry leading tools to help you plan your personal development and advance your career. For more information, please visit our website.

Why subscribe?

- Spend less time learning and more time coding with practical eBooks and Videos from over 4,000 industry professionals

- Improve your learning with Skill Plans built especially for you

- Get a free eBook or video every month

- Mapt is fully searchable

- Copy and paste, print, and bookmark content

packt.com

Did you know that Packt offers eBook versions of every book published, with PDF and ePub files available? You can upgrade to the eBook version at `www.packt.com` and as a print book customer, you are entitled to a discount on the eBook copy. Get in touch with us at `customercare@packtpub.com` for more details.

At `www.packt.com`, you can also read a collection of free technical articles, sign up for a range of free newsletters, and receive exclusive discounts and offers on Packt books and eBooks.

Contributors

About the authors

Ankur Ankan is a BTech graduate from IIT (BHU), Varanasi. He is currently working in the field of data science. He is an open source enthusiast and his major work includes starting pgmpy with four other members. In his free time, he likes to participate in Kaggle competitions.

Abinash Panda has been a data scientist for more than 4 years. He has worked at multiple early-stage start-ups and helped them build their data analytics pipelines. He loves to munge, plot, and analyze data. He has been a speaker at Python conferences. These days, he is busy co-founding a start-up. He has contributed to books on probabilistic graphical models by Packt Publishing.

About the reviewer

Abdullah al Mamun is a professional software engineer and researcher. He has completed his graduation from rajshahi university of engineering & technology (RUET) and BSc in Computer Science and Engineering (CSE). Currently, he is working as a Senior Executive Officer of the Software section in Primeasia University. As a professional software engineer, he has experience in object-oriented design, software architectures, design patterns, test-driven development, and project management. Also, he is interested in research in the fields of artificial intelligence, neural network, pattern recognition, and machine learning. His research has been published in different international journals and conferences, including IEEE.

This Hands-On Markov Models with Python book is a good reference for those involved with teaching and also research and development. In this book, the authors explain the Hidden Markov Model and its real-time application, illustrated with Python source code. I would like to express my gratitude toward the books authors and Packt Publishing for their wonderful collaboration.

Packt is searching for authors like you

If you're interested in becoming an author for Packt, please visit `authors.packtpub.com` and apply today. We have worked with thousands of developers and tech professionals, just like you, to help them share their insight with the global tech community. You can make a general application, apply for a specific hot topic that we are recruiting an author for, or submit your own idea.

Table of Contents

Preface

Using **Hidden Markov Models** (**HMMs**) is a technique for modeling Markov processes with unobserved states. They are a special case of **Dynamic Bayesian Networks** (**DBNs**) but have been found to perform well in a wide range of problems. One of the areas where HMMs are used a lot is speech recognition because HMMs are able to provide a very natural way to model speech data. This book starts by introducing the theoretical aspects of HMMs from the basics of probability theory, and then talks about the different applications of HMMs.

Who this book is for

A basic understanding of probability theory, linear algebra, and calculus will make reading this book a lot easier. For the code examples, basic familiarity with Python programming is expected.

What this book covers

Chapter 1, *Introduction to Markov Process*, starts with a discussion of basic probability theory, and then introduces Markov chains. The chapter also talks about the different types of Markov chain classifying based on continuous or discrete states and time intervals.

Chapter 2, *Hidden Markov Model*, builds on the concept of Markov processes and DBNs to introduce the concepts of the HMM.

Chapter 3, *State Inference – Predicting the States*, introduces algorithms that can be used to predict the states of a defined HMM. The chapter introduces the Forward algorithm, the backward algorithm, the forward-backward algorithm, and the Viterbi algorithm.

Chapter 4, *Parameter Inference Using Maximum Likelihood*, discusses the basics of maximum likelihood learning. The chapter then moves on to applying maximum likelihood learning in the case of HMMs and introduces the Viterbi learning algorithm and Baum-Welch algorithm.

Chapter 5, *Parameter Inference Using Bayesian Approach*, starts by introducing the basic concepts of Bayesian learning. The chapter then applies these concepts in the case of HMMs and talks about the different approximation methods used for learning using the Bayesian method.

Chapter 6, *Time-Series Predicting*, discusses the application of HMMs in the case of time series data. The chapter takes the example of the variation of stock prices and tries to model it using an HMM.

Chapter 7, *Natural Language Processing*, discusses the application of HMMs in the field of speech recognition. The chapter discusses two main areas of application: part-of-speech tagging and speech recognition.

Chapter 8, *2D HMM for Image Processing*, introduces the concept of 2D HMMs and discusses their application in the field of image processing.

Chapter 9, *Markov Decision Process*, introduces the basic concepts of reinforcement learning and then talks about Markov decision process and introduces the Bellman equation to solve them.

To get the most out of this book

You need to have Python 3.4 installed on your machine in order to work through the chapters smoothly.

Download the example code files

You can download the example code files for this book from your account at www.packt.com. If you purchased this book elsewhere, you can visit www.packt.com/support and register to have the files emailed directly to you.

You can download the code files by following these steps:

1. Log in or register at www.packt.com.
2. Select the **SUPPORT** tab.
3. Click on **Code Downloads & Errata**.
4. Enter the name of the book in the **Search** box and follow the onscreen instructions.

Once the file is downloaded, please make sure that you unzip or extract the folder using the latest version of:

- WinRAR/7-Zip for Windows
- Zipeg/iZip/UnRarX for Mac
- 7-Zip/PeaZip for Linux

The code bundle for the book is also hosted on GitHub at `https://github.com/PacktPublishing/Hands-On-Markov-Models-with-Python`. In case there's an update to the code, it will be updated on the existing GitHub repository.

We also have other code bundles from our rich catalog of books and videos available at `https://github.com/PacktPublishing/`. Check them out!

Download the color images

We also provide a PDF file that has color images of the screenshots/diagrams used in this book. You can download it here: `http://www.packtpub.com/sites/default/files/downloads/9781788625449_ColorImages.pdf`.

Conventions used

There are a number of text conventions used throughout this book.

`CodeInText`: Indicates code words in text, database table names, folder names, filenames, file extensions, pathnames, dummy URLs, user input, and Twitter handles. Here is an example: "Now, let's define the `MFCTagger` class."

A block of code is set as follows:

```
from hmmlearn.hmm import GaussianHMM
import numpy as np
import matplotlib.pyplot as plt
```

Any command-line input or output is written as follows:

```
pip install matplotlib datetime
```

Bold: Indicates a new term, an important word, or words that you see onscreen. For example, words in menus or dialog boxes appear in the text like this. Here is an example: "The possible states of the outcomes are also known as the **domain of the random variable**."

Warnings or important notes appear like this.

 Tips and tricks appear like this.

Get in touch

Feedback from our readers is always welcome.

General feedback: If you have questions about any aspect of this book, mention the book title in the subject of your message and email us at customercare@packtpub.com.

Errata: Although we have taken every care to ensure the accuracy of our content, mistakes do happen. If you have found a mistake in this book, we would be grateful if you would report this to us. Please visit www.packt.com/submit-errata, selecting your book, clicking on the Errata Submission Form link, and entering the details.

Piracy: If you come across any illegal copies of our works in any form on the Internet, we would be grateful if you would provide us with the location address or website name. Please contact us at copyright@packt.com with a link to the material.

If you are interested in becoming an author: If there is a topic that you have expertise in and you are interested in either writing or contributing to a book, please visit authors.packtpub.com.

Reviews

Please leave a review. Once you have read and used this book, why not leave a review on the site that you purchased it from? Potential readers can then see and use your unbiased opinion to make purchase decisions, we at Packt can understand what you think about our products, and our authors can see your feedback on their book. Thank you!

For more information about Packt, please visit packt.com.

1
Introduction to the Markov Process

In this chapter, we will develop the basic concepts that we need to understand **Hidden Markov Models (HMM)**. We will cover the following topics:

- Random processes
- Markov processes
- Markov chains or discrete-time Markov processes
- Continuous-time Markov chains

Random variables

As we always do in statistics, let's start with a simple example of rolling a dice. If we consider rolling a fair dice, the outcome of the dice can be anything from 1 to 6, and is random. To represent such situations (the outcome of rolling the dice in this case), in mathematics we use the concept of random variables. We come across a lot of such variables in our everyday lives. Another example could be ordering food at a restaurant. In this case, the outcome could be any food item on the menu. In general terms, a random variable is a variable whose possible values are outcomes of a random phenomenon. The possible states of the outcomes are also known as the **domain of the random variable**, and the outcome is based on the probability distribution defined over the domain of the random variable.

Coming back to rolling the dice, the domain of the random variable outcome, *O*, is given by *domain(O) = (1, 2, 3, 4, 5, 6)*, and the probability distribution is given by a uniform distribution *P(o) = 1/6 ∀ ∈ domain(O)*. Similarly, in the case of the restaurant example, for the random variable *choosing a dish*, the domain would be every item on the menu, and the probability distribution would depend on your food preference. In both of the previous examples, the domain of the random variable has discrete variables; such random variables are known as **discrete random variables**. But it's also possible for the domain to be a continuous space. For example, consider the random variable representing the stock price of Google tomorrow. The domain of this random variable will be all positive real numbers with most of the probability mass distributed around ±5% of today's price. Such random variables are known as **continuous random variables**.

Random processes

In the previous section, we discussed random variables that are able to mathematically represent the outcomes of a single random phenomenon. But what if we want to represent these random events over some period of time or the length of an experiment? For example, let's say we want to represent the stock prices for a whole day at intervals of every one hour, or we want to represent the height of a ball at intervals of every one second after being dropped from some height in a vacuum. For such situations, we would need a set of random variables, each of which will represent the outcome at the given instance of time. These sets of random variables that represent random variables over a period of time are also known as **random processes**. It is worth noting that the domains of all these random variables are the same. Therefore, we can also think of the process as just changing the states.

 Here, we have been talking about random variables at different instances of time, but it doesn't need to be time-based in every case. It could be just some other event. But since, in most cases, it is usually time, and it is much easier to talk about random processes in terms of time, we will use time to represent any such event. The same concepts will apply to creating a model if it varies over some other event instead of time.

Now let's discuss the previous two examples in more detail. Starting with the example of dropping the ball from a height in a vacuum, if we know the exact value of gravity and the height from which the ball is being dropped, we will be able to determine the exact location of the ball at every interval of one second using Newton's laws of motion.

Such random processes, in which we can deterministically find the state of each random variable given the initial conditions (in this case, dropping the ball, zero initial velocity) and the parameters of the system (in this case, the value of gravity), are known as **deterministic random processes** (commonly called **deterministic processes**).

Now let's go to the second example; representing the stock price over time. In this case, even if we know the current price and the exact probability distribution of the price at the next one hour mark, we won't be able to deterministically compute the value. These random processes, in which we can't determine the state of a process, even if we are given the initial conditions and all the parameters of the system, are known as **stochastic random processes** (commonly called **processes**). A very good way of understanding or getting a feel for a stochastic process is to think of it as being the opposite of a deterministic process.

Markov processes

A stochastic process is called a **Markov process** if the state of the random variable at the next instance of time depends only on the outcome of the random variable at the current time. In simplistic mathematical terms, for a stochastic process, $S = \{R1, R_2, \ldots, R_n\} = \{R\}_{t=1, \ldots, n}$, to be a Markov process, it must satisfy the following condition:

$$P(R_{n+1}|R_1, R_2, \ldots, R_n) = P(R_{n+1}|R_n)$$

According to the previous condition, the probability distribution for any variable at any given instance in a Markov process is a conditional distribution, which is conditioned only on the random variable at the last time instance. This property of a system, such that the future states of the system depend only on the current state of the system, is also known as the **Markov property**. Systems satisfying the Markov property are also known as **memoryless systems** since they don't need to remember the previous states to compute the distribution of the next state, or, in other words, the next state depends only on the current state of the system.

A very common example used to explain the Markov process is a drunk man walking along a street. We consider that, since the man is drunk, he can either take a step backward, a step forward, or stay in his current position, which is given by some distribution of these, let's say *[0.4, 0.4, 0.2]*. Now, given the position of the man at any given instance in time, his position at the next instance depends only on his current position and the parameters of the system (his step size and the probability distribution of possible actions). Therefore, this is an example of a Markov process.

In the previous example, let's assume that the drunk man takes an action (steps forward/backward or stays in his position) at fixed intervals of time and his step size is always the same. With these considerations, the Markov process in our example has a discrete state space. Also, since the man takes steps after fixed intervals of time, we can think of it as a discrete time. But Markov processes don't need to have discrete state space or discrete time intervals. Considering discrete and continuous time as well as discrete and continuous state space, we can categorize Markov processes into four main categories:

- Discrete time and discrete state space
- Discrete time and continuous state space
- Continuous time and discrete state space
- Continuous time and continuous state space

We will discuss each of these categories of Markov process in more detail in the following sections.

Installing Python and packages

Before moving ahead, we need to set up Python and all the packages required to run the code examples. For all the code examples in this book, we will be using Python 3.4. All the example code in the book is also available on GitHub at `https://github.com/PacktPublishing/HandsOnMarkovModelswithPython`. We highly recommend using Miniconda to set up your environment for running the examples. Miniconda can be downloaded from `https://conda.io/miniconda.html`.

Installation on Windows

Miniconda can be installed on a Windows system by just double-clicking on the downloaded `.exe` file and following the installation instructions. After installation, we will need to create a `conda` environment and install all the required packages in the environment. To create a new Python 3.4 environment with the name `hmm`, run the following command:

```
conda create -n hmm python=3.4
```

After creating the environment, we will need to activate it and install the required packages in it. This can be done using the following commands:

```
activate hmm
conda install numpy scipy
```

Installation on Linux

On Linux, after downloading the `Miniconda` file, we will need to give it execution permissions and then install it. This can be done using the following commands:

```
chmod +x Miniconda.sh
./Miniconda.sh
```

After executing the file, we can simply follow the installation instructions. Once installed, we will need to create a new environment and install the required packages. We can create a new Python 3.4 environment with the name hmm using the following commands:

```
conda create -n hmm python=3.4
```

Once the environment has been created, we will need to activate it and install the packages inside it using the following:

```
source activate hmm
conda install numpy scipy
```

Markov chains or discrete-time Markov processes

A Markov chain is a type of Markov process in which the time is discrete. However, there is a lot of disagreement among researchers on what categories of Markov process should be called **Markov chain**. But, most commonly, it is used to refer to discrete-state-space Markov processes. Therefore, a Markov chain is a stochastic process over a discrete state space satisfying the Markov property. More formally, we can say that a discrete-time Markov chain is a sequence of random variables $X_1, X_2, X_3, \ldots$ that satisfy the Markov property, namely that the probability of moving from the current state to the next state depends only on the present state and not on any of the previous states. In terms of the probability distribution, we can say that, given that the system is at time instance n, the conditional distribution of the states at the next time instance, $n + 1$, is conditionally independent of the state of the system at time instances *{1, 2, . . ., n-1}*, given the state of the random variable at time instance n. This can be written as follows:

$$Pr(X_{n+1} = x | X_1 = x_1, X_2 = x_2, \ldots, X_n = x_n) = Pr(X_{n+1} = x | X_n = x_n)$$

Markov chains are often represented using directed graphs. The nodes in the directed graphs represent the different possible states of the random variables, and the edges represent the probability of the system going from one state to the other in the next time instance. Let's take a simple example of predicting the weather to understand this representation better. We will consider that there are three possible states of the random variable *Weather={Sunny, Rainy, Snowy}*, and possible Markov chains for this can be represented as shown in *Figure 1.1*:

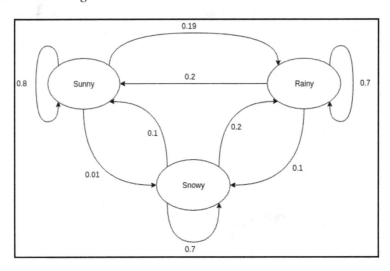

Figure 1.1: A simple Markov chain on the random variable, representing the random variable Weather={Sunny, Rainy, Snowy} and showing the probability of the random variable switching to other states in the next time instance

One of the main points to understand in Markov chains is that we are modeling the outcomes of a sequence of random variables over time. This is sometimes confusing for people since the model is represented using a single graph, which doesn't mention anything about time. So, the name state transitions is not a particularly good name for this, since the state is not changing for any random variable; rather, we are trying to determine the state of the next random variable given the observed state of our current random variable. Coming back to our example, we can see that the nodes of the graph represent the different possible states of the random variable *Weather,* and the edges between them show the probability of the next random variable taking the different possible states, given the state of the current random variable. The self-loops show the probability of the model staying in its current state. In the previous Markov chain, let's say we know that the observed state of the current random variable is *Sunny,* then the probability that the random variable at the next time instance will also take the value *Sunny* is *0.8*. It could also take the value *Rainy* with a probability of *0.19*, or *Snowy* with a probability of *0.01*. One thing to note here is that the sum of all the probability values on all the outward edges from any state should equal 1, since it's an exhaustive event.

Now, let's try to code this simple Markov chain. We will start by defining a simple
MarkovChain class, and we will keep on adding methods to this class as we go through
this chapter:

```python
import numpy as np

class MarkovChain(object):
    def __init__(self, transition_prob):
        """
        Initialize the MarkovChain instance.

        Parameters
        ----------
        transition_prob: dict
            A dict object representing the transition probabilities in
            Markov Chain. Should be of the form: {'state1': {'state1':
            0.1, 'state2': 0.4}, 'state2': {...}}
        """
        self.transition_prob = transition_prob
        self.states = list(transition_prob.keys())

    def next_state(self, current_state):
        """
        Returns the state of the random variable at the next time
        instance.

        Parameters
        ----------
        current_state: str
            The current state of the system.
        """
        return np.random.choice(
            self.states, p=[self.transition_prob[current_state][next_state]
                            for next_state in self.states])

    def generate_states(self, current_state, no=10):
        """
        Generates the next states of the system.

        Parameters
        ----------
        current_state: str
            The state of the current random variable.

        no: int
            The number of future states to generate.
        """
        future_states = []
```

```
for i in range(no):
    next_state = self.next_state(current_state)
    future_states.append(next_state)
    current_state = next_state
return future_states
```

Now, we can try out our example with this `MarkovChain` class:

```
>>> transition_prob = {'Sunny': {'Sunny': 0.8, 'Rainy': 0.19,
 'Snowy': 0.01},
 'Rainy': {'Sunny': 0.2, 'Rainy': 0.7,
 'Snowy': 0.1},
 'Snowy': {'Sunny': 0.1, 'Rainy': 0.2,
 'Snowy': 0.7}}

>>> weather_chain = MarkovChain(transition_prob=transition_prob)
>>> weather_chain.next_state(current_state='Sunny')
'Sunny'
>>> weather_chain.next_state(current_state='Snowy')
'Snowy'
>>> weather_chain.generate_states(current_state='Snowy', no=10)
['Snowy', 'Snowy', 'Snowy', 'Rainy', 'Snowy', 'Snowy', 'Rainy',
 'Rainy', 'Snowy', 'Snowy']
```

 In the previous code example, you might find your outputs to be different from what's shown here. This is because the Markov chain is probabilistic in nature and it picks on the next state based on a probability distribution, which can give different outputs on different runs.

So far in the discussion, we have considered that the probability space of the variables doesn't change over different instances of time. This is known as a **time-homogeneous Markov chain**, but it is also possible to have a **time-inhomogeneous Markov chain**, which also has a lot of applications but is outside the scope of this book.

Parameterization of Markov chains

In the code for the Markov chain in the previous section, we used a dictionary to parameterize the Markov chain that had the probability values of all the possible state transitions. Another way of representing state transitions is using a **transition matrix**. The transition matrix, as the name suggests, uses a tabular representation for the transition probabilities. The transition matrix for the example in *Figure 1.1* is shown in the following table.

The following table shows the transition matrix for the Markov chain shown in *Figure 1.1*. The probability values represent the probability of the system going from the state in the row to the states mentioned in the columns:

States	Sunny	Rainy	Snowy
Sunny	0.8	0.19	0.01
Rainy	0.2	0.7	0.1
Snowy	0.1+	0.2	0.7

The transition matrix represents the same information as in the dictionary, but in a more compact way. For this reason, the transition matrix is the standard way of representing Markov chains. Let's modify our `MarkovChain` class so that it can accept a transition matrix:

```python
import numpy as np

class MarkovChain(object):
    def __init__(self, transition_matrix, states):
        """
        Initialize the MarkovChain instance.

        Parameters
        ----------
        transition_matrix: 2-D array
            A 2-D array representing the probabilities of change of
            state in the Markov Chain.

        states: 1-D array
            An array representing the states of the Markov Chain. It
            needs to be in the same order as transition_matrix.
        """
        self.transition_matrix = np.atleast_2d(transition_matrix)
        self.states = states
        self.index_dict = {self.states[index]: index for index in
                           range(len(self.states))}
        self.state_dict = {index: self.states[index] for index in
                           range(len(self.states))}

    def next_state(self, current_state):
        """
        Returns the state of the random variable at the next time
        instance.

        Parameters
        ----------
```

```
            current_state: str
                The current state of the system.
            """
            return np.random.choice(
                        self.states,
    p=self.transition_matrix[self.index_dict[current_state], :])

        def generate_states(self, current_state, no=10):
            """
            Generates the next states of the system.

            Parameters
            ----------
            current_state: str
                The state of the current random variable.

            no: int
                The number of future states to generate.
            """
            future_states = []
            for i in range(no):
                next_state = self.next_state(current_state)
                future_states.append(next_state)
                current_state = next_state
            return future_states
```

Running this code should also give similar results to what we got in the previous section. Using a transition matrix might not seem like a good idea because it requires us to create extra variables to store the indices. But, in cases when we have hundreds of states, using a transition matrix is much more efficient than using the simple dictionary implementation. In the case of a transition matrix, we can simply use NumPy indexing to get the probability values in the next_state method, whereas we were looping over all the state names in the previous implementation:

```
>>> transition_matrix = [[0.8, 0.19, 0.01],
                         [0.2,  0.7,  0.1],
                         [0.1,  0.2,  0.7]]
>>> weather_chain = MarkovChain(transition_matrix=transition_matrix,
                                states=['Sunny', 'Rainy', 'Snowy'])
>>> weather_chain.next_state(current_state='Sunny')
'Sunny'
>>> weather_chain.next_state(current_state='Snowy')
'Sunny'
>>> weather_chain.generate_states(current_state='Snowy', no=10)
['Snowy', 'Rainy', 'Rainy', 'Rainy', 'Rainy', 'Rainy',
 'Rainy', 'Rainy', 'Sunny', 'Sunny']
```

Properties of Markov chains

In this section, we will talk about the different properties of Markov chains, namely reducibility, periodicity, transience and recurrence, ergodicity, and steady-state analysis and limiting distributions. We will also try some simple examples of our `MarkovChain` class to show these properties.

Reducibility

A Markov chain is said to be **irreducible** if we can reach any state of the given Markov chain from any other state. In terms of states, state j is said to be **accessible** from another state i if a system that started at state i has a non-zero probability of getting to the state j. In more formal terms, state j is said to be accessible from state i if an integer $n_{ij} \geq 0$ exists such that the following condition is met:

$$Pr(X_{n_{ij}} = j | X_0 = i) = p_{ij}^{n_{ij}} > 0$$

The n_{ij} here is basically the number of steps it takes to go from state i to j, and it can be different for different pairs of values for i and j. Also, for a given state i, if all the values for $n_{ij} = 0$, it means that all the states of the Markov chain are directly accessible from it. The accessibility relation is reflexive and transitive, but not necessary symmetric. We can take a simple example to understand this property:

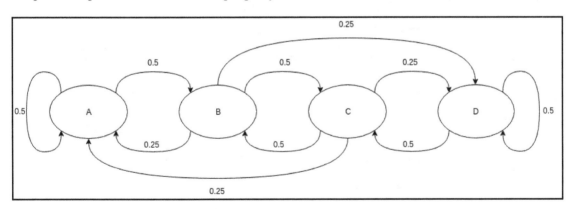

Figure 1.2: An example of an irreducible Markov chain

In the previous example, it can be clearly seen that all of the states are accessible from all other states and hence are irreducible.

Note in the examples in *Figure 1.2* and *Figure 1.3* that we haven't represented edges if probability values are 0. This helps to keep the model less complicated and easier to read.

In the following example, we can see that state **D** is not accessible from **A**, **B**, or **C**. Also, state **C** is not accessible from either **A** or **B**. But all the states are accessible from state **D**, and states **A** and **B** are accessible from **C**:

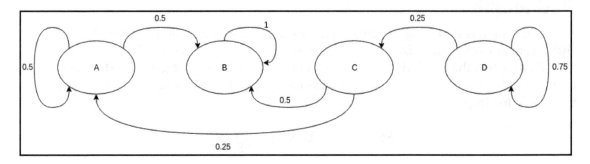

Figure 1.3: An example of a reducible Markov chain

We can also add a couple of methods to our `MarkovChain` class to check which states in our chain are reachable and whether our chain is irreducible:

```
from itertools import combinations

def is_accessible(self, i_state, f_state):
    """
    Check if state f_state is accessible from i_state.

    Parameters
    ----------
    i_state: str
        The state from which the accessibility needs to be checked.
    f_state: str
        The state to which accessibility needs to be checked.
    """
    reachable_states = [i_state]
    for state in reachable_states:
        if state == self.index_dict[f_state]:
            return True
        else:
            reachable_states.append(np.nonzero(
                self.transition_matrix[self.index_dict[i_state], :])[0])
    return False
```

```
def is_irreducible(self):
    """
    Check if the Markov Chain is irreducible.
    """
    for (i, j) in combinations(self.states, self.states):
        if not self.is_accessible(i, j):
            return False
    return True
```

Let's give our examples a try using the examples in *Figure 1.2* and *Figure 1.3*:

```
>>> transition_irreducible = [[0.5, 0.5, 0, 0],
                              [0.25, 0, 0.5, 0.25],
                              [0.25, 0.5, 0, 0.25],
                              [0, 0, 0.5, 0.5]]
>>> transition_reducible = [[0.5, 0.5, 0, 0],
                            [0, 1, 0, 0],
                            [0.25, 0.5, 0, 0],
                            [0, 0, 0.25, 0.75]]
>>> markov_irreducible =
MarkovChain(transition_matrix=transition_irreducible,
                            states=['A', 'B', 'C', 'D'])
>>> markov_reducible = MarkovChain(transition_matrix=transition_reducible,
                            states=['A', 'B', 'C', 'D'])
>>> markov_irreducible.is_accessible(i_state='A', f_state='D')
True
>>> markov_irreducible.is_accessible(i_state='B', f_state='D')
True
>>> markov_irreducible.is_irreducible()
True
>>> markov_reducible.is_accessible(i_state='A', f_state='D')
False
>>> markov_reducible.is_accessible(i_state='D', f_state='A')
True
>>> markov_reducible.is_accessible(i_state='C', f_state='D')
False
>>> markov_reducible.is_irreducible()
False
```

Periodicity

State i is said to have period k if any possible path to return to state i would be a multiple of k steps. Formally, it is defined like this:

$$k = \gcd\{n > 0 : Pr(X_n = i | X_0 = i) > 0\}$$

Here, *gcd* means the **greatest common divisor** (**GCD**). Basically, k is the GCD of the length/number of steps of all possible paths from state i back to itself. If there are no possible paths from state i back to itself, then the period for it is not defined. We also need to note that k has nothing to do with the number of steps required to return to the starting state. For example, let's say that for any given state the number of steps required to return to it are *(4, 6, 8, 12, 16)*. In this case *k=2*, but the minimum number of steps required to return is 4, and 2 doesn't even appear in the list of possible numbers of steps.

For any given state in the Markov chain, if *k=1*, the state is said to be **aperiodic**. A Markov chain is called aperiodic if all of its states are aperiodic. One major thing to note is that, in the case of an irreducible Markov chain, a single aperiodic state is enough to imply that all the states are aperiodic. Let's take a simple example and check the periodicity of different states:

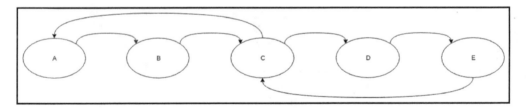

Figure 1.4: Markov chain is also periodic

In the previous example, we can easily see that for state **A** the possible paths to return are **A -> B -> C -> A** or **A -> B -> C -> D -> E -> C -> A**. For these two paths, the path lengths are 3 and 6, respectively, and hence state **A** has a period of 3. Similarly, **B**, **C**, **D**, and **E** also each has a period of 3 in the Markov chain, and hence the Markov chain is also periodic:

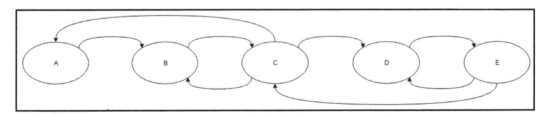

Figure 1.5: Example of Markov Chain with aperiodic states.

In this example, we added a couple of extra edges, due to which the possible path lengths for **A** are now 3, 5, 7, ...; and for **B** are 2, 3, 4, 5, ... And, since the GCD of these path lengths is 1, states **A** and **B** are both now aperiodic. Similarly, we can compute the period of other nodes, each of which is also 1, and hence the Markov chain is also aperiodic.

Let's now add a couple of new methods to our `MarkovChain` class to compute the period of different states and check whether our model is aperiodic:

```
def get_period(self, state):
    """
    Returns the period of the state in the Markov Chain.

    Parameters
    ----------
    state: str
        The state for which the period needs to be computed.
    """
    return gcd([len(i) for i in all_possible_paths])

def is_aperiodic(self):
    """
    Checks if the Markov Chain is aperiodic.
    """
    periods = [self.get_period(state) for state in self.states]
    for period in periods:
        if period != 1:
            return False
    return True
```

Let's now try out our methods on our examples. In this example, we will randomly assign probability values to different transitions:

```
>>> transition_periodic = [[0, 1, 0, 0, 0],
                           [0, 0, 1, 0, 0],
                           [0.5, 0, 0, 0.5, 0],
                           [0, 0, 0, 0, 1],
                           [0, 0, 1, 0, 0]]
>>> transition_aperiodic = [[0, 1, 0, 0, 0],
                            [0, 0, 1, 0, 0],
                            [0.5, 0.25, 0, 0.25, 0],
                            [0, 0, 0, 0, 1],
                            [0, 0, 0.5, 0.5, 0]]
>>> markov_periodic = MarkovChain(transition_matrix=transition_periodic,
                        states=['A', 'B', 'C', 'D', 'E'])
>>> markov_aperiodic = MarkovChain(transition_matrix=transition_aperiodic,
                        states=['A', 'B', 'C', 'D', 'E'])
```

```
>>> markov_periodic.get_period('A')
3
>>> markov_periodic.get_period('C')
3
>>> markov_aperiodic.is_periodic()
False

>>> markov_aperiodic.get_period('A')
1
>>> markov_aperiodic.get_period('B')
1
>>> markov_aperiodic.is_periodic()
True
```

Transience and recurrence

Given that we start at state i, it is called **transient** if there is a non-zero probability that we will never return to state i. To define this in more formal terms, let's consider a random variable T_i as the first return time to state i:

$$T_i = \{n \geq 1 : X_n = i | X_0 = i\}$$

Let's now define another term, f_{ii}^n, as the probability of the system returns to state i after n steps:

$$f_{ii}^n = Pr(T_i = n)$$

Now we can define that any given state i is transient if the following condition is met:

$$Pr(T_i < \infty) = \sum_{n=1}^{\infty} f_{ii}^n < 1$$

In the preceding equation, we are basically checking whether the total sum of probabilities of returning to state i in step sizes less than ∞ is less than 1. If the total sum is less than 1, it would mean that the probability of T_i to be ∞ is greater than 0 which would mean that the state i is transient. The given state i is called **recurrent** if it is not transient:

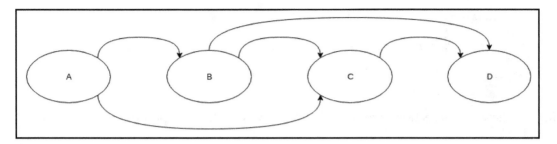

Figure 1.6:

In the preceding example, we can see that states **A** and **B** are transient because **A** doesn't have any incoming edge. **B** does have an incoming edge, but it's incoming from another transient state and therefore it is also transient. Hence, once the system leaves state **A** or **B**, it won't be able to come back.

It is really simple to check whether a given state is transient or not. We can simply check whether there are any incoming edges from other states or not. If not, the state is transient. Let's write a simple method to check this for our `MarkovChain` class:

```
def is_transient(self, state):
    """
    Checks if a state is transient or not.

    Parameters
    ----------
    state: str
        The state for which the transient property needs to be checked.
    """
    if all(self.transition_matrix[~self.index_dict[state],
self.index_dict[state]] == 0):
        return True
    else:
        return False
```

Now we can use this method in our example in *Figure 1.6* to check which nodes are transient:

```
>>> transient_matrix = [[0, 0.5, 0.5, 0],
                        [0, 0, 0.25, 0.75],
                        [0, 0, 0, 1],
                        [0, 0, 0.5, 0.5]]
>>> transient_markov = MarkovChain(transition_matrix=transient_matrix,
                        states=['A', 'B', 'C', 'D'])
```

```
>>> transient_markov.is_transient('A')
True
>>> transient_markov.is_transient('B')
True
>>> transient_markov.is_transient('C')
False
```

In the following subsections, we will talk about the statistical properties of the random variable T_i.

Mean recurrence time

The first-return time for the initial state i is also known as the **hitting time**. It was represented using the random variable T_i in the previous section. The **mean recurrence time** of state i is defined as its expected return time:

$$M_i = E[T_i] = \sum_{n=1}^{\infty} f_{ii}^n$$

If the mean recurrence time, M_i, is finite, the state is called **positive recurrent**, otherwise it is called **null recurrent**.

Expected number of visits

As is evident from the name, the **expected number of visits** for any state i is the number of times the system is expected to be in that state. Also, a given state i is recurrent if and only if the expected number of visits to i is infinite:

$$\sum_{n=0}^{\infty} p_{ii}^n = \infty$$

Absorbing states

State i is said to be an **absorbing state** if it is impossible for a system to leave that state once it reaches it. For a state to be an absorbing state, the probability of staying in the same state should be *1*, and all the other probabilities should be *0*:

$$p_{ii} = 1 \, and \, p_{ij} = 0 \, for \, i \neq j$$

In a Markov chain, if all the states are absorbing, then we call it an absorbing Markov chain:

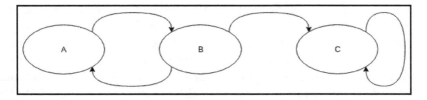

Figure 1.7: An example showing an absorbing state C, since the probability of transitioning from state C to C is *1*

Again, we can add a very simple method to check for absorbing states in our `MarkovChain` class:

```python
def is_absorbing(self, state):
    """
    Checks if the given state is absorbing.

    Parameters
    ----------
    state: str
    The state for which we need to check whether it's absorbing
    or not.
    """
    state_index = self.index_dict[state]
    if self.transition_matrix[state_index, state_index]
```

We can again check whether our state in the example is absorbing by creating a Markov chain and using the `is_absorbing` method:

```python
>>> absorbing_matrix = [[0, 1, 0],
                        [0.5, 0, 0.5],
                        [0, 0, 1]]
>>> absorbing_chain = MarkovChain(transition_matrix=absorbing_matrix,
                                  states=['A', 'B', 'C'])
>>> absorbing_chain.is_absorbing('A')
False
>>> absorbing_chain.is_absorbing('C')
True
```

Ergodicity

State i is said to be ergodic if it is recurrent, has a period of 1, and has a finite mean recurrence time. If all the states of a Markov chain are ergodic, then it's an ergodic Markov chain. In general terms, a Markov chain is ergodic if there is a number N, such that any state in the system can be reached from any other state in any number of steps greater than or equal to the number N. Therefore, in the case of a fully connected transition matrix, where all transitions have a non-zero probability, this condition is fulfilled with $N=1$.

Steady-state analysis and limiting distributions

In a Markov chain, vector π is called the **stationary distribution** if $\forall\, j \in s$ satisfies the following conditions:

$$0 < \pi_j < 1$$

$$\sum_{j \in S} \pi_j = 1$$

$$\pi_j = \sum_{i \in S} \pi_i p_{ij}$$

The stationary distribution is one of the most important properties of Markov chains, and we will talk about it in much more detail in later sections of this chapter.

Continuous-time Markov chains

Continuous-time Markov chains are quite similar to discrete-time Markov chains except for the fact that in the continuous case we explicitly model the transition time between the states using a positive-value random variable. Also, we consider the system at all possible values of time instead of just the transition times.

Exponential distributions

The random variable x is said to have an exponential distribution with a rate of distribution of λ if its probability density function is defined as follows:

$$f_X(x|\lambda) = \begin{cases} \lambda e^{-\lambda x} & \text{for } x > 0, \\ 0 & \text{for } x \leq 0 \end{cases}$$

Here, the rate of distribution λ needs to be greater than 0. We can also compute the expectation of X as this:

$$
\begin{aligned}
E[X] &= \int_0^\infty x\lambda e^{-\lambda x}\, dx \\
&= \left[\frac{-xe^{-\lambda x}}{\lambda} \Big|_0^\infty + \frac{1}{\lambda} \int_0^\infty e^{-\lambda x}\, dx \right] \\
&= \lambda \left[0 + \frac{1}{\lambda} \frac{-e^{-\lambda x}}{\lambda} \Big|_0^\infty \right] \\
&= \lambda \frac{1}{\lambda^2} = \frac{1}{\lambda}
\end{aligned}
$$

We see that the expectation of X is inversely proportional to the rate of learning. This means that an exponential distribution with a higher rate of learning would have a lower expectation. The exponential distribution is often used to model problems that involve modelling time until some event happens. A simple example could be modelling the time before an alarm clock goes off, or the time before a server comes to your table in a restaurant. And, as we know $E[X] = \frac{1}{\lambda}$, the higher the learning rate, the sooner we would expect the event to happen, and hence the name *learning rate*.

We can also compute the second moment and the variance of the exponential distribution:

$$E[X^2] = \int_0^\infty x^2 \lambda e^{-\lambda x}\, dx = \frac{2}{\lambda^2}$$

And, using the first moment and the second moment, we can compute the variance of the distribution:

$$Var(X) = E[X^2] - E[X]^2$$
$$= \frac{2}{\lambda^2} - \frac{1}{\lambda^2} = \frac{1}{\lambda^2}$$

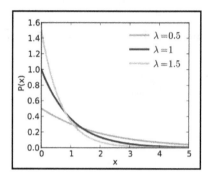

Figure 1.x: Probability distribution of exponential distribution

$$\lambda e^{-\lambda x} \; \forall x \geq 0$$

Now we will move on to some of the properties of the exponential distribution that are relevant to our example:

- **Memoryless**: *Figure 1.x* shows a plot of an exponential distribution. In the diagram, we can clearly see that the graph after any given point (*a* in this case) is an exact copy of the original distribution. We can also say that an exponential distribution that is conditioned on $(X > a)$ still stays exponential. If we think about this property in terms of our examples, it means that if we had an alarm clock, and at any time, *t*, we check that it still hasn't gone off, we can still determine the distribution over the time ahead of *t*, which will be the same exponential distribution. This property of the exponential distribution is known as being **memoryless**, since at any given point in time, if you know the current state of the system (in this example, that the alarm hasn't gone off), you can determine the probability distribution over time in the future. This property of exponential distributions is quite similar to Markov chains, as you may recall from previous sections.

- **Probability of minimum value**: Let's say we have n independent exponential distributions over the random variables $X_0, \ldots, X_n$ with learning rates $\lambda_0, \ldots, \lambda_n$, respectively. For these distributions, we can prove that the distribution of $min(X_0, \ldots, X_n)$ is also an exponential distribution with learning rate $\sum_{i=0}^{n} \lambda_i$:

$$P(min(X_0, \ldots, X_n) > t) = P(X_0 > t, \ldots, X_n > t)$$
$$= \prod_{i=0}^{n} P(X_i > t)$$
$$= \prod_{i=0}^{n} e^{-\lambda_i t}$$
$$= e^{-(\lambda_0 + \lambda_1 + \ldots + \lambda_n)t}$$

We will use both of these properties of the exponential distribution in our example for the continuous time Markov chain in a later section.

Poisson process

The Poisson process is a continuous process, and there can be multiple interpretations of it, which lead to different possible definitions. In this section, we will start with the formal definition and build up to a more simple, intuitive definition. A continuous-time stochastic process $N(t):t > 0$ is a **Poisson process** with a rate $\lambda > 0$ if the following conditions are met:

- $N(0) = 0$
- It has **stationary** and **independent increments**
- The distribution of $N(t)$ is Poisson with mean λt:

$$P(N(t) = k) = \frac{(\lambda t)^k}{k!} e^{-\lambda t} \quad \text{for } k = 0, 1, 2, \ldots$$

First of all, we need to define what the stationary and independent increments are. For a continuous-time stochastic process, $X(t): \geq 0$, an increment is defined as the difference in state of the system between two time instances; that is, given two time instances s and t with $s < t$, the increment from time s to time t is $X(t) - X(s)$. As the name suggests, a process is said to have a stationary increment if its distribution for the increment depends only on the time difference.

In other words, a process is said to have a stationary increment if the distribution of $X(t_1) - X(s_1)$ is equal to $X(t_2) - X(s_2)$ if $t_1 > s_1, t_2 > s_2$ and $t_1 - s_1 = t_2 - s_2$. A process is said to have an independent increment if any two increments in disjointed time intervals are independent; that is, if $t_1 > s_1 > t_2 > s_2$, then the increments $X(t_2) - X(s_2)$ and $X(t1) - X(s1)$ are independent.

Now let's come back to defining the Poisson process. The Poisson process is essentially a counting process that counts the number of events that have occurred before time t. This count of the number of events before time t is given by $N(t)$, and, similarly, the number of events occurring between time intervals t and $t + s$ is given by $N(t + s) - N(t)$. The value $N(t + s) - N(t)$ is Poisson-distributed with a mean λ_s. We can see that the Poisson process has stationary increments in fixed time intervals, but as $t \to \infty$, the value of $N(t)$ will also approach infinity; that is, $N(t) \to \infty$. Another thing worth noting is that, as the value of λ increases, the number of events happening will also increase, and that is why λ is also known as the **rate of the process**.

This brings us to our second simplified definition of the Poisson process. A continuous-time stochastic process $N(t): t \geq 0$ is called a Poisson process with the rate of learning $\lambda > 0$ if the following conditions are met:

- $N(0) = 0$
- It is a counting process; that is, $N(T)$ gives the count of the number of events that have occurred before time t
- The times between the events are distributed independently and identically, with an exponential distribution having a learning rate of λ

Continuous-time Markov chain example

Now, since we have a basic understanding of exponential distributions and the Poisson process, we can move on to the example to build up a continuous-time Markov chain. In this example, we will try to show how the properties of exponential distributions can be used to build up generic continuous-time Markov chains. Let's consider a hotel reception where n receptionists are working in parallel. Also consider that the guests arrive according to a Poisson process, with rate λ, and the service time for each guest is represented using an exponential random variable with learning rate μ. Also, if all the receptionists are busy when a new guest arrives, he/she will depart without getting any service. Now let's consider that a new guest arrives and finds all the receptionists are busy, and let's try to compute the expected number of busy receptionists in the next time interval.

Let's start by assuming that T_k represents the number of k busy receptionists in the next time instance. We can also use T_k to represent the expected number of busy receptionists found by the next arriving guest if k receptionists are busy at the current time instance. These two representations of T_k are equivalent because of the memoryless property of exponential distributions.

Firstly, T_0 is clearly 0, because if there are currently 0 busy receptionists, the next arrival will also find 0 busy receptionists for sure. Now, considering T_1, if there are currently i busy receptionists, the next arriving guest will find 1 busy receptionist if the time to the next arrival is less than the remaining service time for the busy receptionist. From the memoryless property, we know that the next arrival time is exponentially distributed with a learning rate of λ, and the remaining service time is also exponentially distributed with a learning rate of μ. Therefore, the probability that the next guest will find one receptionist busy is $\frac{\lambda}{\lambda + \mu}$ and hence the following is true:

$$T_1 = (1)\frac{\lambda}{\lambda + \mu} + (0)\frac{\mu}{\lambda + \mu} = \frac{\lambda}{\lambda + \mu}$$

In general, we consider the situation that k receptionists are busy. We can obtain an expression for T_k by conditioning on what happens first. When we have k receptionists busy, we can think of basically $k+1$ independent exponential distributions: k exponentials with a learning rate of μ for the remaining service time for each receptionist, and 1 exponential distribution with a learning rate of λ for the next arriving guest. In our case, we want to condition on whether a service completion happens first or a new guest arrives first. The time for a service completion will be the minimum of the k exponentials. This first completion time is also exponentially distributed with a learning rate of $k\mu$. Now, the probability of having a service completion before the next guest arrives is $\frac{k\mu}{(\lambda + k\mu)}$.
Similarly, the probability of the next thing happening being a guest arrival is $\frac{\lambda}{(\lambda + k\mu)}$.

Now, based on this, we can say that if the next event is service completion, then the expected number of busy receptionists will be T_{k-1}. Otherwise, if a guest arrives first, there will be k busy receptionists. Therefore we have the following:

$$T_k = T_{k-1}\frac{k\mu}{k\mu + \lambda} + k\frac{\lambda}{k\mu + \lambda}$$

We need to just solve this recursion now. T_2 will be given by this equation:

$$T_2 = T_1 \frac{2\mu}{2\mu + \lambda} + \frac{2\lambda}{2\mu + \lambda}$$
$$= \left(\frac{\lambda}{\lambda + \mu} \right) \frac{2\mu}{2\mu + \lambda} + \frac{2\lambda}{2\mu + \lambda}$$

If we continue this same pattern, we will get T_3 as follows:

$$T_3 = T_2 \frac{3\mu}{3\mu + \lambda} + \frac{3\lambda}{3\lambda + \mu}$$
$$= \left(\frac{2\mu}{2\mu + \lambda} \right) \frac{3\mu}{3\mu + \lambda} + \frac{3\lambda}{3\mu + \lambda}$$

We can see a pattern in the values of T_1 and T_2, and therefore we can write a general term for it as follows:

$$T_n = \frac{n\lambda}{n\mu + \lambda} + \sum_{i=1}^{n-1} \frac{i\lambda}{i\mu + \lambda} \prod_{j=i+1}^{n} \frac{j\mu}{j\mu + \lambda}$$

Let's point out our observations on the previous example:

- At any given time instance, if there are i busy receptionists, for $i < n$ there are $i + 1$ independent exponential distributions, with i of them having rate μ, and 1 of them having rate λ. The time until the process makes a jump is exponential, and its rate is given by $i\mu + \lambda$. If all the receptionists are busy, then only the n exponential distributions corresponding to the service time can trigger a jump, and the time until the process makes a jump is exponential with rate $n\mu$.
- When the process jumps from state i, for $i < n$, it jumps to state $i + 1$ with probability $\frac{\lambda}{(i\mu + \lambda)}$, and jumps to state $i - 1$ with probability of $\frac{n\mu}{n\mu} = 1$.
- When the process makes a jump from state i, we can start up a whole new set of distributions corresponding to the state we jumped to. This is because, even though some of the old exponential distributions haven't triggered, it's equivalent to resetting or replacing those distributions.

Every time we jump to state i, regardless of when the time is, the distribution of how long we stay in state i and the probabilities of where we jump to next when we leave state i are the same. In other words, the process is time-homogeneous.

The preceding description of a continuous-time stochastic process corresponds to a continuous-time Markov chain. In the next section, we will try to define it in a more formal way.

Continuous-time Markov chain

In the previous section, we showed an example of a continuous-time Markov chain to give an indication of how it works. Let's now move on to formally define it. In a continuous-time Markov chain with a discrete state space S, for each state $i \in S$ we have an associated set of n_i independent exponential distributions with rates $q_i, j_1, ..., q_i, j_{n_i}$, where $j_1, ..., j_{n_i}$ is the set of possible states the process may jump to when it leaves state i. And, when the process enters state i, the amount of time it spends in state i is exponentially distributed with rate $v_i =$

$$q_{i,j_1} + ... + q_i j_{n_i},$$ and when it leaves state i it will go to state j_l with probability $\dfrac{q_{i,j_l}}{v_i}$ for $l = 1, ..., n_i$.

We can also extend the Markov property from the discrete-time case to continuous time.

For a continuous-time stochastic process $(X(t) : t \geq 0)$ with state space S, we say it has the Markov property if the following condition is met:

$$P(X(t) = j | X(s) = i, X(t_{n-1}) = i_{n-1}, ..., X(t_1) = i_1)$$
$$= P(X(t) = j | X(s) = i),$$

Here, $0 \leq t_1 \leq t2 \leq ....t_{n-1} \leq s \leq t$ is any non-decreasing sequence of $n + 1$ times, and $i_{1,}i2, ..., i_{n-1}, i, j \in S$ are any $n + 1$ states in the state space, for any integer $n \geq 1$.

Similarly, we can extend time-homogeneity to the case of continuous-time Markov chains. We say that a continuous-time Markov chain is time homogenous if, for any $s \leq t$, and any states $i, j \in S$, the following condition is met:

$$P(X(t) = j | X(s) = i) = P(X(t - s) = j | X(0) = i)$$

As in the case of discrete-time Markov chains, a continuous-time Markov chain does not need to be time-homogeneous, but non-homogeneous Markov chains are out of scope for this book. For more details on non-homogeneous Markov chains, you can refer to Cheng-Chi Huang's thesis on the topic: `https://lib.dr.iastate.edu/cgi/viewcontent.cgi?article=8613context=rtd`.

Now let's define the transition probability for a continuous-time Markov chain. Just as the rates q_{ij} in a continuous-time Markov chain are the counterpart of the transition probabilities p_{ij} in a discrete-time Markov chain, there is a counterpart to the n-step transition probabilities $p_{ij}(t)$ for a time-homogeneous, continuous-time Markov chain, which is defined as follows:

$$P_{ij}(t) = P(X(t) = j | X(0) = i)$$

Summary

In this chapter, we gave a detailed introduction to Markov chains. We talked about different types of Markov chains, mainly chains with a discrete state space, with either discrete time or continuous time. We also introduced the concepts of time-homogeneous and non-time-homogeneous Markov chains. We discussed the different properties of Markov chains in detail, and provided relevant examples and code.

Markov chains and their properties are the basic concepts on which HMMs are built. In the next chapter, we will discuss HMMs in much more detail.

2
Hidden Markov Models

In the previous chapter, we discussed Markov chains, which are helpful in modelling a sequence of observations across time. In this chapter, we are going to study the **Hidden Markov Model** (**HMM**), which is also used to model sequential data but is much more flexible than Markov chains.

In this chapter, we will cover the following topics:

- Markov models
- The HMM
- Evaluation of an HMM
- Extensions of HMM

Markov models

The Markov model is a stochastic model in which the state of the random variable at the next instance of time depends only on the outcome of the random variable at the current time. The simplest kind of Markov model is a Markov chain, which we discussed in Chapter 1, *Introduction to Markov Process*.

Suppose we have a set of sequential observations $(x_1, \ldots, x_n)$ obeying the Markov property, then we can state the joint probability distribution for N observations as the following:

$$Pr(x_1, \ldots, x_N) = Pr(x_1) \prod_{n=2}^{N} Pr(x_n | x_{n-1})$$

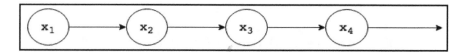

Graphical representation of a first-order Markov chain in which the distribution of the current observation is conditioned on the value of the previous observation

The preceding representation of the Markov chain is different from the representations we saw earlier. In this representation, the observations are presented as nodes and the edges represent conditional probability between two observations, namely $Pr(x_n | x_{n-1})$. This is how probabilistic graphical models are generally represented, where nodes represent random variables and edges represent a conditional probability distribution between these two variables. This graphical representation gives us insight into the causal relationships between random variables.

State space models

We can see that a simple Markov chain is very restrictive and does not work well for situations where we anticipate that several successive observations will provide important information required to predict the next observation. Fortunately, a Markov chain can be tweaked to support these cases as well:

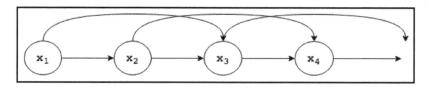

Second-order Markov chain in which the distribution of the current observation is conditioned on the values of the last two observations

Let's consider a Markov chain where the probability of the next state not only depends on the current state but also on the last state. This type of Markov chain is called a **second-order Markov chain** and the joint probability distribution can be represented as follows:

$$Pr(\mathbf{x}_1, \ldots, \mathbf{x}_n) = Pr(\mathbf{x}_1) Pr(\mathbf{x}_2 | \mathbf{x}_1) \prod_{n=3}^{N} Pr(\mathbf{x}_n | \mathbf{x}_{n-1}, \mathbf{x}_{n-2})$$

Using the d-separation property, we see that the conditional distribution of X_n given X_{n-1} and X_{n-2} is independent of all observations, $X_1, \ldots, X_{n-3}$.

Similarly, we can extend this to an Mth-order Markov chain in which the conditional distribution for a particular observation depends on the previous M observations. However, we are now paying the price of a large number of parameters for increased flexibility.

Suppose that the observations are discrete variables having K states. Then the conditional distribution, $Pr(X_n | X_{n-1})$, in a first-order Markov chain will be specified by a set of $K-1$ parameters for each of the K states of X_{n-1}, giving a total of $K(K-1)$ parameters. If we extend this to an Mth-order Markov chain, where joint distribution is built up from conditionals, $Pr(x_n | x_{n-M} \ldots, x_{n-1})$, the number of parameters in such a model would have $K^{M-1}(K-1)$. Because this grows exponentially with M, it will often render this approach impractical for larger values of M. But, what if we want to build a model for sequential data that is not bounded by any order of Markov assumption, and yet it can be represented by a limited number of parameters?

Such models can be created by introducing latent (or hidden) variables. Latent variables allow us to create a rich class of models constructed out of simple components. Let's assume that for each observation, x_n, we have a latent variable, z_n (which may or may not have the same dimensionality as the observed variable). If these latent variables form a first-order Markov chain, this type of model can be called a **state space model**, which is represented in the following diagram:

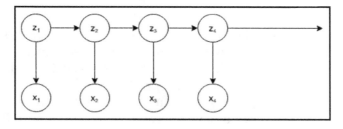

State space model representing a distribution, where each observation is conditioned upon a latent variable

Using the d-separation property, we can see that there is always a path between any two observed variables, x_n and x_m, via latent variables and this path can never be blocked. So the $Pr(x_{n+1} | x_1, \ldots, x_n)$ distribution for observation x_{n+1} given all previous observations does not exhibit any conditional independence properties, and thus the prediction for x_{n+1} depends on all previous observations.

As the latent variables form a Markov chain, they satisfy the following conditional distribution:

$$z_{n+1} \perp\!\!\!\perp z_{n-1} | z_n$$

Thus, the joint distribution of this model can be stated as follows:

$$Pr(x_1, \ldots, x_N, z_1, \ldots, z_N) = Pr(z_1) \left[\prod_{n=2}^{N} Pr(z_n | z_{n-1}) \right] \prod_{m=1}^{N} Pr(x_m | z_m)$$

The HMM

An HMM is a specific case of state space model in which the latent variables are discrete and multinomial variables. From the graphical representation, we can also consider an HMM to be a double stochastic process consisting of a hidden stochastic Markov process (of latent variables) that we cannot observe directly, and another stochastic process that produces a sequence of the observation given the first process.

Before moving on to the parameterization, let's consider an example of coin-tossing to get an idea of how it works. Assume that we have two unfair coins, M_1 and M_2, with M_1 having a higher probability (70%) of getting heads and M_2 having a higher probability (80%) of getting tails. Someone sequentially flips these two coins, however, we do not know which one. We can only observe the outcome, which can either be heads (H) or tails (T):

$$H, T, H, H, T, T, H, T, H$$

We can consider the unfair coin selected to be the latent variable, and the outcome of the coin toss to be the observed data. To predict the next outcome sequence of observation, we would at least require information such as which coin was selected at first, the next coin to flip given the previous one, and the probability of getting H or T given the coin. Assuming that both of the coins have equal priority of getting selected at first and each coin is equally likely to get selected given the previous coin selected, we can create the following state diagram:

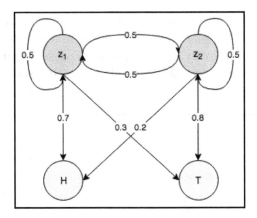

State diagram for coin toss HMM

In the previous diagram, z_1 and z_2 represent states of the latent variable coin selected (z_1 representing coin M_1 getting selected, and z_2 representing coin M_2 being selected). The arcs represent transition probabilities of moving from one state of latent variable to the other and the straight lines represent the probabilities of the observed variable (toss outcome) given the latent variable (coin selected).

Parameterization of HMM

In the previous section, we saw an example of an HMM to get an idea of how the model works. Let's now formally parameterize an HMM.

As the latent variables of an HMM are discrete multinomial variables, we can use the 1-of-K encoding scheme to represent it, where the z_n variable is represented by a K-dimensional vector of binary variables, $z_{nk} \in \{0,1\}$, such that $z_{nk} = 1$ and $z_{nj} = 0$ for $j \neq k$ if the z_n variable is in the k state.

With this in mind, we can create a matrix with the transition probability matrix A, where A_{ij} = $Pr(Z_{nj} = 1 | z_{n-1}, i = 1)$. As the A_{ij} represent the probability of moving from state i to state j, it holds the property of $\sum_{j=1}^{K} A_{ij} = 1$ and can be expressed using the $K(K-1)$ parameters. Thus we can represent the conditional probability distribution as follows:

$$Pr(z_n | z_{n-1}, \mathbf{A}) = \prod_{i=1}^{K} \prod_{j=1}^{K} Aij^{z_{nj} z_{n-1,i}}$$

The transition matrix is generally represented using a state-transition diagram, as we saw in `Chapter 1`, *Introduction to Markov Process*. But we can take the same representation and unfold it across time to get a *lattice* or *trellis* diagram, as presented in the following image. We will be using this representation of HMM in the following sections for learning parameters and making inferences from the model:

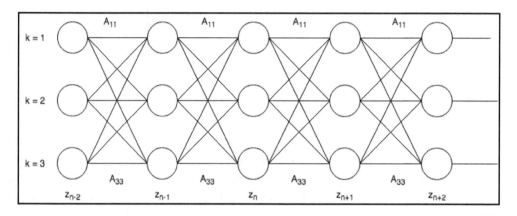

Trellis diagram for an HMM with latent variables with three states

As the initial latent node, z_1, does not have a parent node, it has a marginal distribution, $Pr(z_1)$, which can be represented by a vector of probabilities, π, such that $\pi_k = Pr(z_{1k} = 1)$ with $\sum_{k=1}^{K} \pi_k = 1$. Thus, the probability of $Pr(z_1 | \pi)$ can be expressed as follows:

$$Pr(z_1 | \pi) = \prod_{k=1}^{K} \pi_k^{z_{1k}}$$

The third and final parameter required to parameterize an HMM is the conditional probability of the observed variable given the latent variable, namely the emission probability. It is represented by the conditional distribution, $Pr(x_n | z_n, \Phi)$, which is governed by some parameters, Φ. If the observed variable, x_n, is discrete, the emission probability may take the form of a conditional probability table (multinomial HMM). Similarly, if the observed variable, x_n, is continuous, then this distribution might be a Gaussian distribution (Gaussian HMM) where $\phi = \{\mu, \sigma\}$ denotes the set of parameters governing the distribution, namely the mean and variance.

Thus, the joint probability distribution over both the latent and observed variables can be stated as follows:

$$P(\mathbf{X}, \mathbf{Z}|\theta) = P(\mathbf{z}_1|\pi) \left[\prod_{n=2}^{N} P(\mathbf{z}_n|\mathbf{z}_{n-1}, \mathbf{A}) \right] \prod_{m=2}^{N} P(\mathbf{x}_m|\mathbf{z}_m, \phi)$$

Here, $X = \{x_1, ..., x_N\}$, $Z = \{z_1, ..., z_N\}$ and $\theta = \{A, \pi, \Phi\}$ denotes the set of parameters governing the model.

An HMM model is called a **homogenous model** when all the conditional distributions governing the latent variables share the same transition matrix, A, and all the emission probabilities share the same parameters, Φ.

Now, let's try to code a simple multinomial HMM. We will start by defining a simple `MultinomialHMM` class and keep on adding methods as we move forward:

```
import numpy as np

class MultinomialHMM:
  def __init__(self, num_states, observation_states, prior_probabilities,
  transition_matrix, emission_probabilities):
  """

Initialize Hidden Markov Model

Parameters
-----------
num_states: int
Number of states of latent variable
observation_states: 1-D array
An array representing the set of all observations
prior_probabilities: 1-D array
An array representing the prior probabilities of all the states
of latent variable
        transition_matrix: 2-D array
            A matrix representing the transition probabilities of change of
            state of latent variable
        emission_probabilities: 2-D array
            A matrix representing the probability of a given observation
            given the state of the latent variable
    """
    # As latent variables form a Markov chain, we can use
    # use the previous defined MarkovChain class to create it
    self.latent_variable_markov_chain = MarkovChain(
```

```
        transition_matrix=transition_matrix,
        states=['z{index}'.format(index=index) for index in
range(num_states)],
        )
    self.observation_states = observation_states
    self.prior_probabilities = np.atleast_1d(prior_probabilities)
    self.transition_matrix = np.atleast_2d(transition_matrix)
    self.emission_probabilities = np.atleast_2d(emission_probabilities)
```

Using the `MultinomialHMM` class, we can define the HMM coin that we discussed previously as follows:

```
coin_hmm = MultinomialHMM(num_states=2,
                          observation_states=['H', 'T'],
                          prior_probabilities=[0.5, 0.5],
                          transition_matrix=[[0.5, 0.5], [0.5, 0.5]],
                          emission_probabilities=[[0.8, 0.2], [0.3, 0.7]])
```

Generating an observation sequence

For a given HMM parameterized by $\{A, \pi, \Phi\}$, we can generate a sequence of observations, $\{x_1, ..., x_N\}$, using the following steps:

1. Set $n = 1$
2. Choose an initial state of the latent variable, z_1, according to the prior distribution, π
3. Choose an observation, x_1, for the given value of z_1, by sampling the emission-probability distribution governed by Φ
4. Transit to the next state of the latent variable, z_{n+1}, according to the state-transition probability matrix, A
5. Set $n = n + 1$ and repeat step 3 if $n \leq N$, otherwise terminate

We can add a method to generate samples in the previously defined `MultinomialHMM` class, as follows:

```
def observation_from_state(self, state):
    """
    Generate observation for a given state in accordance with
    the emission probabilities

    Parameters
    ----------
    state: int
```

```
            Index of the current state
        """
        state_index = self.latent_variable_markov_chain.index_dict[state]
        return np.random.choice(self.observation_states,
                                p=self.emission_probabilities[state_index, :])

def generate_samples(self, no=10):
    """
    Generate samples from the hidden Markov model

    Parameters
    ----------
    no: int
        Number of samples to be drawn

    Returns
    -------
    observations: 1-D array
        An array of sequence of observations

    state_sequence: 1-D array
        An array of sequence of states
    """
    observations = []
    state_sequence = []

    initial_state =
np.random.choice(self.latent_variable_markov_chain.states,
                                p=self.prior_probabilities)

    state_sequence.append(initial_state)
    observations.append(self.observation_from_state(initial_state))

    current_state = initial_state
    for i in range(2, no):
        next_state =
self.latent_variable_markov_chain.next_state(current_state)
        state_sequence.append(next_state)
        observations.append(self.observation_from_state(next_state))
        current_state = next_state

    return observations, state_sequence
```

We can use the `generate_samples` method on our HMM coin example to generate an observation sequence:

```
>>> coin_hmm.generate_samples()
(['T', 'H', 'H', 'T', 'T', 'H', 'H', 'H', 'H'], ['z1', 'z0', 'z0', 'z1',
'z1', 'z0', 'z1', 'z1', 'z1'])
```

Installing Python packages

HMM can also have a Gaussian distribution for the emission probability. Just like `MultinomialHMM`, we can also sample from `GaussianHMM`. In the next code example, we use the `GaussianHMM` class provided in the `hmmlearn` library to see how the samples are generated from this type of model:

```
source activate hmm
conda install scikit-learn
pip install hmmlearn
```

Once the Python packages are installed, we can use the following code to generate samples from Gaussian HMM:

```
from hmmlearn.hmm import GaussianHMM
import numpy as np
import matplotlib.pyplot as plt

startprob = np.array([0.6, 0.3, 0.1, 0.0])
# The transition matrix, note that there are no transitions possible
# between component 1 and 3
transmat = np.array([[0.7, 0.2, 0.0, 0.1],
                     [0.3, 0.5, 0.2, 0.0],
                     [0.0, 0.3, 0.5, 0.2],
                     [0.2, 0.0, 0.2, 0.6]])
# The means of each component
means = np.array([[0.0,  0.0],
                  [0.0, 11.0],
                  [9.0, 10.0],
                  [11.0, -1.0]])
# The covariance of each component
covars = .5 * np.tile(np.identity(2), (4, 1, 1))

# Build an HMM instance and set parameters
model = hmm.GaussianHMM(n_components=4, covariance_type="full")

# Instead of fitting it from the data, we directly set the estimated
# parameters, the means and covariance of the components
model.startprob_ = startprob
```

```
model.transmat_ = transmat
model.means_ = means
model.covars_ = covars

X, state_sequence = model.sample(n_samples=100)

plt.plot(X[:, 0], X[:, 1], ".-", label="observations", ms=6,
         mfc="orange", alpha=0.7)
for i, m in enumerate(means):
    plt.text(m[0], m[1], 'Component %i' % (i + 1),
             size=12, horizontalalignment='center',
             bbox=dict(alpha=.7, facecolor='w'))
plt.legend(loc='best')
plt.show()
```

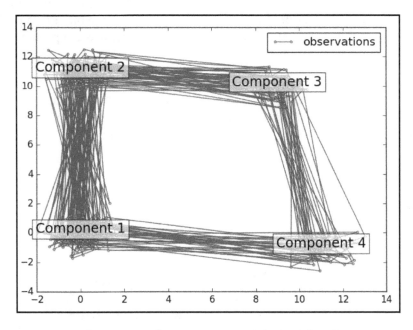

Sampling from an HMM with a four-state latent variable, z, and a Gaussian emission model, p(x|z)

Evaluation of an HMM

In the previous section, we discussed generating an observation sequence of a given HMM. But, in reality, most of the time we are not interested in generating the observation sequence, mostly because we don't know the parameters of the HMM to generate observations in the first place.

For a given HMM representation, in most of the applications, we are always trying to address the following three problems:

- **Evaluation of the model**: Given the parameters of the model and the observation sequence, estimating the probability of the sequence
- **Predicting the optimal sequence**: Given the parameters of the model and the observation sequence, estimating the most probable sequence of the state sequence that had produced these observations
- **Parameter-learning**: Given a sequence of observations, estimating the parameters of the HMM model that generated it

In this section, we'll discuss the first problem, the evaluation of the model, and in the following chapters, we will discuss the other two problems in detail. As we will see in the later chapters, evaluating the model forms the basis for solving the other two problems. Thus, solving this problem efficiently is the first stepping stone toward parameter-learning and inference.

Let's formally describe the problem of model evaluation. Given an HMM parameterized by $\theta = \{A, \pi, \Phi\}$ and an observation sequence, $X = \{x_1, ..., x_N\}$, we need to compute the probability of $Pr(X|\theta)$. From our discussions in the previous section, we can say that we can compute $Pr(X|\theta)$ by marginalizing the joint-probability distribution $Pr(X, Z|\theta)$, where $Z = \{z_1, ..., z_N\}$, with respect to Z:

$$Pr(\mathbf{X}|\theta) = \sum_{\mathbf{Z}} Pr(\mathbf{X}, \mathbf{Z}|\theta)$$

In the previous section, we saw that the following is true:

$$Pr(\mathbf{X}, \mathbf{Z}|\theta) = Pr(z_1|\pi) \left[\prod_{n=2}^{N} Pr(z_n|z_{n-1}, \mathbf{A}) \right] \prod_{m=2}^{N} Pr(x_m|z_m, \phi)$$

$$= \pi_1 Pr(x_1|z_1, \phi) A_{12} Pr(x_2|z_2, \phi) \ldots A_{n-1,n} Pr(x_n|z_n, \phi)$$

Thus the $Pr(X, Z|\theta)$ probability can be stated as follows:

$$Pr(\mathbf{X}, \mathbf{Z}|\theta) = \sum_{\mathbf{Z}} \pi_1 Pr(x_1|z_1, \phi) A_{12} Pr(x_2|z_2, \phi) \ldots A_{n-1,n} Pr(x_n|z_n, \phi)$$

For a model with K states and an observation length of N, there are K^T possible state sequences. Each term in the summation requires $2N$ operations. As a result, the evaluation becomes a mathematical operation of the order of $2N$ X K^T. For example, if we consider a model with five states, $K = 5$, and an observation sequence of length $N = 100$, the number of required operations is of the order of 10^{72}, which makes this method of evaluation intractable even for a very small HMM.

Extensions of HMM

In the previous sections, we discussed HMM, sampling from it and evaluating the probability of a given sequence given its parameters. In this section, we are going to discuss some of its variations.

Factorial HMMs

Let's consider the problem of modelling of several objects in a sequence of images. If there are M objects with K different positions and orientations in the image, there are be K^M possible states for the system underlying an image. An HMM would require K^M distinct states to model the system. This way of representing the system is not only inefficient but also difficult to interpret. We would prefer that our HMM could capture the state space by using M different K-dimensional variables.

A factorial HMM is such a representation. In this model, there are multiple independent Markov chains of latent variables and the distribution of the observed variable at any given time is conditional on the states of all the corresponding latent variables in that given time. The graphical model of the system can be represented as follows:

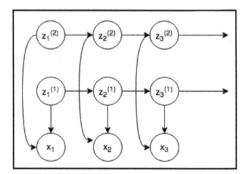

A factorial HMM comprising two Markov chains

The motivation for considering factorial HMM can be seen by noting that in order to represent, say, 10 bits of information at a given time step, a standard HMM would need $K = 2^{10} = 1024$ latent states, whereas a factorial HMM could make use of 10 binary latent chains. However, this presents additional complexity in training, as we will see in the later chapters.

Tree-structured HMM

In the previous section, we discussed factorial HMM, in which the latent variables formed independent Markov chains. This independence assumption about the latent variables can be relaxed by introducing some coupling between them. One way to couple latent variables is to order them such that $z_n^{(m)}$ depends on $z_n^{(l)}$ for all $1 \leq l \leq m$. Furthermore, if all the output variables and the latent variables depend on some random input variable, x_n, we obtain a tree-structured HMM represented as follows:

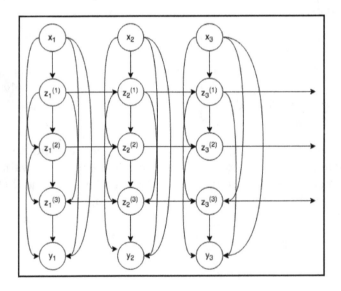

Graphical representation of a tree-structured HMM

The architecture of this model can be interpreted as a probabilistic decision tree. Let's considered at first-time slice $n=1$, and try to understand how this model would generate data. Based on the value of x_1, the top node, $z_1^{(1)}$, can take K values (assuming that the hidden variables have K states). This partitions the x space into K decision groups. The next node, $z_1^{(2)}$, further partitions into K subregions, and so on. The output, y_1, is generated from the input, x_1, and K-way decisions at each node. At the next time slice, the same thing is going to happen, expect that each decision in the tree depends on the decision taken at that node in the previous time slice. Therefore, this model can be interpreted as a probabilistic decision tree with Markovian dynamics.

Summary

In this chapter, we got a detailed introduction to Markov model and HMM. We talked about parameterizing an HMM, generating samples from it, and their code. We discussed estimating the probability of observation, which would form the basis of inference, which we'll cover in the next chapter. We also talked about various extensions of HMMs.

In the next chapter, we will take an in-depth look at inference in HMMs.

State Inference - Predicting the
States

3

In the previous chapters, we introduced Markov chains and the **Hidden Markov Model** (**HMM**), and saw examples of modeling problems using them. In this chapter, we will see how we can make predictions using these models or ask the models questions (known as **inference**). The algorithms used for computing these values are known as **inference algorithms**. In this chapter, we will specifically look into computing probability distribution over the state variables.

This chapter will cover the following topics:

- State inference in HMM
- Dynamic programming
- Forward-backward algorithm
- Viterbi algorithm

State inference in HMM

Let's start with a simple example to show what kind of interesting questions we can ask our HMM models. We are taking an example of *robot localization*. There are a lot of variations of this example, but we are assuming that a robot is moving in a 2D grid, as shown in *Figure 3.1*. The robot also has four sensors on it. Each of these sensors detects whether there's a wall right next to the robot in the sensor's direction.

We would like to model the movement of the robot in the following grid along with the observations from our sensors:

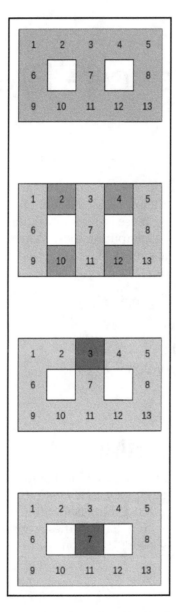

Figure 3.1: The probability distribution of the position of the robot over time

In *Figure 3.1*, we see how the observations at different time instances change the probability of the location of the robot in the grid. Initially, we start with a uniform probability over all the positions in the grid. Now, at time *t=1*, let's say the sensors of our robot show that there are walls on the top and bottom sides. Having this observation will change our perception of the location of the robot. Now we will have a higher probability of the robot being in either blocks 2, 4, 10, or 12, as shown in the second block in *Figure 3.1*. If we are at time instance *t=2*, our robot's sensors say that there is a wall only at the top, we will have the highest probability of it being in block 3, as shown in the third block in *Figure 3.1*. This is because we knew its last most probable position and, when combining that information with the current sensor readings, block 3 is the robot's likely location. Now, if we are at time *t=3*, the robot's sensors indicate there are walls on the left and right, then it would mean that the robot is most likely in in block 7. This process enables us able to locate the position of our robot in the grid based on just the sensor readings over time.

Since we are modelling the transition of state (position in the grid) of the robot over some duration of time along with an outcome at each instance (sensor output), HMM seems to be the perfect model in the situation. In this example, we are assuming that we know the transition probability of the robot's position. We are also assuming that we know the structure of the grid and therefore we will know the emission probabilities. We can use the emission probability to also model the uncertainty in the output of the sensors since they might give noise results at some instance:

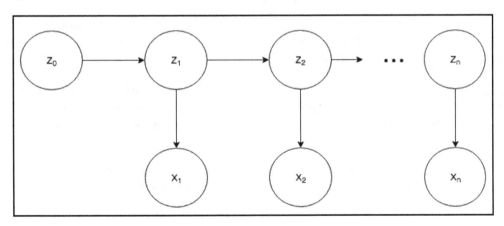

Figure 3.2: An example HMM for the robot localization

Now let's think about the kind of questions we might want to ask our model. We might be interested in knowing the position of our robot at any time instance given all the observations till that time instance. Another question that we might want to ask is the probability of our sensor output at some time instance given all the positions of the robot until that time instance. We might also be interested in computing the joint distribution over our observed variables and the position of the robot. All these values can be easily computed using the *forward algorithm, backward algorithm, or forward-backward algorithm*.

Now, instead of asking for distributions, we might be interested in the most probable path the robot took. To compute the most probable path, we would need to do a MAP inference over the state at each time instance of the robot. This can be done efficiently using the Viterbi algorithm.

In the following sections, we will introduce these algorithms formally and see how we can implement them. All of these algorithms rely on a very important programming paradigm known as **dynamic programming**. Dynamic programming allows us to run these inference algorithms in HMMs in tractable time. We will discuss dynamic programming in detail in the next section.

Dynamic programming

Dynamic programming is a programming paradigm in which we divide a complex problem into smaller sub-problems. We solve these sub-problems and store the results. Whenever we need to recompute the same sub-problem again, we just used our stored results, thus saving us computation time at the expense of using storage space. This technique of caching the results of sub-problems is known as **memoization**. Therefore, using dynamic programming allows us to speed up our computations by using memoization, and in some cases, it can bring the computational complexity from exponential to linear, as we will see in the following example.

One of the simplest examples of optimization using dynamic programming is computing the nth member of the Fibonacci sequence. Any term in a Fibonacci sequence is the sum of the last two terms, which can be formally defined as follows:

$$fib(0)=0$$

$$fib(1)=1$$

$$fib(n)=fib(n-1)+fib(n-2)$$

Here, *fib(n)* represents the nth number in the Fibonacci sequence. From the definition, we can easily compute the Fibonacci sequence as: *0, 1, 1, 2, 3, 5, 8, 13*.

Now let's say we want to write a function which would return the nth number in the Fibonacci sequence. A simple way to write this function could be to use recursion, as shown in the following code:

```
def fibonacci(n):
    """
    Returns the n-th number in the Fibonacci sequence.

    Parameters
    ----------
    n: int
        The n-th number in the Fibonacci sequence.
    """
    if n <= 1:
        return n
    else:
        return fibonacci(n-1) + fibonacci(n-2)
```

In the preceding code, we have a simple if ... else condition, where if n is less than or equal to 1, we return the value of n; otherwise, we use recursion to compute the sum of the previous two numbers in the sequence. Now let's try to determine the number of calls to the fibonacci function for a small n, let's say 5. Our function calls would look something like the following:

```
fibonacci(5) = fibonacci(4) + fibonacci(3)
fibonacci(5) = (fibonacci(3) + fibonacci(2)) + (fibonacci(2) +
fibonacci(1))
fibonacci(5) = ((fibonacci(2) + fibonacci(1)) + (fibonacci(1) +
fibonacci(0))) + ((fibonacci(1) + fibonacci(0)) + fibonacci(1))
fibonacci(5) = (((fibonacci(1) + fibonacci(0)) + fibonacci(1)) +
(fibonacci(1) + fibonacci(0))) + ((fibonacci(1) + fibonacci(0)) +
fibonacci(1))
```

For such a small value of n, we can still see the repetition in the number of calls to the function with the same argument. We can see that fibonacci(1) is being called five times and fibonacci(0) is getting called three times. If we move a level up, we can see that fibonacci(2) is also getting called multiple times. In this case, the computation is still tractable, but for large values of n the run time of this function would grow exponentially; the runtime complexity is given by $O(2^n)$. To give an idea of how fast the runtime grows, to compute the 1,000[th] term in the Fibonacci sequence using this algorithm, we would need more time than the age of our universe on a computer built with all the electrons in our observable universe.

Since we have proved that it is impossible to compute the nth term of the Fibonacci sequence for any moderately large n, we will look at another algorithm that is based on dynamic programming and looks as follows:

```python
cache = {0: 0, 1: 1} # Initialize the first two values.
def fibonacci(n):
    """
    Returns the n-th number in the Fibonacci sequence.

    Parameters
    ----------
    n: int
        The n-th number in the Fibonacci sequence.
    """
    try:
        return cache[n]
    except KeyError:
        fib = fibonacci(n-1) + fibonacci(n-2)
        cache[n] = fib
        return fib
```

In this case, we are storing the result of each of our calls to the function in a dictionary, which allows us to access it in $O(1)$. Because of this cache, we only need to compute each term of the Fibonacci sequence exactly once. For each call, we first check whether we have already computed the value. If we have already computed it, we directly access it from the dictionary, otherwise we compute the value. The runtime complexity of this algorithm is $O(n)$ since we are computing each term in the sequence exactly once. We can see, therefore, that using dynamic programming facilitates a trade-off between the runtime complexity and memory complexity, and this allows us to bring down the runtime complexity from being exponential to linear.

If we think about the way we have programmed the Fibonacci series, we start with trying to compute the nth number and then compute the values we are missing. This can be thought of as a top-down approach. Another approach could be a bottom-up approach, in which we start by computing the 0th term and then move to the first, second, and so on. The concept of dynamic programming is the same in both cases, but with just a minor difference in how we write the code, shown as follows:

```python
cache = [0, 1]   # Initialize with the first two terms of Fibonacci series.
def fibonacci(n):
    """
    Returns the n-th number in the Fibonacci sequence.

    Parameters
    ----------
    n: int
```

```
    The n-th number in the Fibonacci sequence.
"""
for i in range(2, n):
    cache.append(cache[i-1] + cache[i-2])
return cache[-1]
```

As you can see, the code in the preceding example is much simpler, and we don't need to check whether we have already computed the values. This works well in problems where we need all the previous values to compute the next value. However, if we don't need all the previous values, we will end up computing unnecessary values with the bottom-up approach.

We will see in the next sections that the inference algorithms in HMMs allow us to use dynamic programming to break the problem into sub-problems, which makes computations tractable.

Forward algorithm

Let's now formally define our problem for the forward algorithm. In the case of the forward algorithm, we are trying to compute the joint distribution of the position of the robot at any time instance using the output of the sensors till that time instance, as shown in the following diagram:

Forward algorithm: $P(Z_k, X_{1:k})$

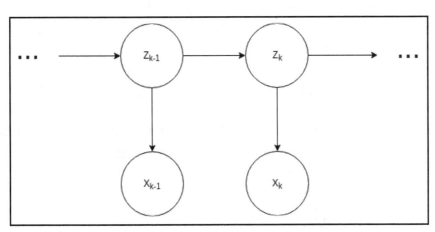

Figure 3.3: HMM showing two time slices, *k-1* and *k*

To compute this probability distribution, we will try to split the joint distribution term into smaller known terms. As we will see, we can write a recursion formula over time for the distribution. We start by introducing a new variable, Z_{k-1}, in the distribution, $P(Z_k, X_{1:k})$, as follows:

$$P(Z_k, X_{1:k}) = \sum_{Z_{k-1}=1}^{m} P(Z_k, Z_{k-1}, X_{1:k})$$

The marginalization rule of probability is:
$$P(x) = \sum_y P(x, y)$$
The product rule of probability is:
$$P(x, y) = P(x|y)P(y)$$

Here, we are basically using the *marginalization* rule of probability to introduce Z_{k-1} and then summing its states. In this case, we have assumed that Z_{k-1} has m states, so now we can use the *product* rule of probability to split this term as follows:

$$P(Z_k, X_{1:k}) = \sum_{Z_{k-1}} P(X_k|Z_k, Z_{k-1}, X_{1:k-1})P(Z_k|Z_{k-1}, X_{1:k-1})P(Z_{k-1}, X_{1:k-1})$$

In the last chapter, we saw how the d-separation property of HMM can make variables independent from each other. Here, we will apply some of those conditions to simplify our terms in the preceding equation. As we know that, given the hidden state, the observation is independent of all the terms in previous time instances, we also know: $X_k \perp (Z_{k-1}, X_{1:k-1})|Z_k$. Applying this to the first term of our preceding equation, we can write it as the following:

$$P(X_k|Z_k, Z_{k-1}, X_{1:k-1}) = P(X_k|Z_k)$$

Similarly, we know that the current hidden state is dependent on the last hidden state and is independent of hidden states before that. Hence, in this case, the formula is $Z_k \perp X_{1:k-1}|Z_{k-1}$. Using this property, we can write our second term in the equation as follows:

$$P(Z_k|Z_{k-1}, X_{1:k-1}) = P(Z_k|Z_{k-1})$$

Now, if we compare our last term with the term we were trying to compute, we should see there is a similarity between them. Let's define a new function, α, as follows:

$$\alpha(k) = P(Z_k, X_{1:k})$$

Now we can rewrite our original equation as the following:

$$\alpha(k) = \sum_{Z_{k-1}} P(X_k|Z_k)P(Z_k|Z_{k-1})\alpha(k-1)$$

So, we now have a nice recursive equation and we are familiar with all the terms in the equation. The first term, $P(X_k|Z_k)$, is the emission probability of the HMM. The second term of the equation, $P(Z_k|Z_{k-1})$, is the transition probability and is also known. Now we can focus on solving this recursive equation. When solving any recursive equation, we need to know at least one of the values, so we can start computing consecutive terms. In this case, we know the value of $\alpha(1)$, which is given as follows:

$$\alpha(1) = P(Z_1, X_1)$$
$$= P(Z_1)P(X_1|Z_1)$$

Here, $P(Z_1)$ is the initial probability of the position of the robot, which we know, and $P(X_1|Z_1)$ is the emission probability of HMM, which is also known. Using these two values, we can compute the value of $\alpha(1)$. Once we have the value of $\alpha(1)$, we can use our recursive equation to compute all the α values.

Now let's talk about the computational complexity of this algorithm to see whether the inference is tractable. As we can see in the equation for computing each α, we are doing a sum over all the states of Z_{k-1}, and we have assumed that it has m states; for each one of these steps, we do m multiplications for computing $P(X_k|Z_k)P(Z_k|Z_{k-1})\alpha(k-1)$. Therefore, to compute the next α, we do m^2 computations. If we want to compute $\alpha(n)$, we will need nm^2 computations, which gives us the computational complexity of the algorithm as $O(nm^2)$.

Let's now try to write the code for our robot localization problem to compute the joint distribution using the forward algorithm. For simplicity, let's assume that we have only one sensor on the robot that checks whether there is a wall on the left-hand side of the robot. To define the model, we mainly need two quantities: the transition matrix and the emission matrix. In our example, we assume that the robot can either stay at its original position or move a block in any possible direction in any given time instance. Therefore, if the robot is at position 1 at any given time, it can be in positions 1, 2, or 6 at the next time instance with equal probabilities of *0.33*.

In this way, we can write the transition probability from state 1 as:

$$t_1 = [0.33, 0.33, 0, 0, 0, 0.33, 0, 0, 0, 0, 0, 0, 0]$$

In a similar way, we can write the transition probabilities, $P(Z_{t+1} | Z_t)$, from each of the position, and we will get the following transition matrix:

```
import numpy as np

transition_matrix = np.array([[0.33, 0.33,     0,     0,    0, 0.33,     0,
0,     0,     0,     0,     0,    0],
                [0.33, 0.33, 0.33,     0,    0,     0,     0,     0,     0,     0,
0,     0,    0],
                [   0, 0.25, 0.25, 0.25,    0,     0, 0.25,     0,     0,     0,
0,     0,    0],
                [   0,    0, 0.33, 0.33, 0.33,     0,     0,     0,     0,     0,
0,     0,    0],
                [   0,    0,    0, 0.33, 0.33,     0,     0, 0.33,     0,     0,
0,     0,    0],
                [0.33,    0,    0,    0,    0, 0.33,     0,     0, 0.33,     0,
0,     0,    0],
                [   0,    0, 0.33,    0,    0,     0, 0.33,     0,     0;     0,
0.33,     0,    0],
                [   0,    0,    0,    0, 0.33,     0,     0, 0.33,     0,     0,
0,     0, 0.33],
                [   0,    0,    0,    0,    0, 0.33,     0,     0, 0.33, 0.33,
0,     0,    0],
                [   0,    0,    0,    0,    0,     0,     0,     0, 0.33, 0.33,
0.33,     0,    0],
                [   0,    0,    0,    0,    0,     0,     0,     0,     0, 0.33,
0.33, 0.33,    0],
                [   0,    0,    0,    0,    0,     0,     0,     0,     0,     0,
0.33, 0.33, 0.33],
                [   0,    0,    0,    0,    0,     0,     0, 0.33,     0,     0,
0, 0.33, 0.33]])
```

Coming to the emission probability in this problem, $P(X_t | Z_t)$, we should have the emission probability of 1 for the states that have a wall on their left. Hence, the emission probability would be as follows:

```
emission = np.array([1.0, 0.0, 0.0, 0.0, 0.0, 1.0, 1.0, 1.0, 1.0, 0.0, 0.0,
0.0, 0.0])
```

However, as we don't know the position of our robot at *t=0*, we will assume that it has a uniform distribution over all the possible states. Therefore, the initial probability, $P(Z_0)$, can be written as follows:

```
init_prob = np.array([0.077, 0.077, 0.077, 0.077, 0.077, 0.077, 0.077,
                      0.077, 0.077, 0.077, 0.077, 0.077, 0.077])
```

With these values in hand, we should be able to run the forward algorithm, but before that, we need to code up the algorithm, as follows:

```
def forward(obs, transition, emission, init):
    """
    Runs forward algorithm on the HMM.

    Parameters
    ----------
    obs:        1D list, array-like
                The list of observed states.

    transition: 2D array-like
                The transition probability of the HMM.
                size = {n_states x n_states}

    emission:   1D array-like
                The emission probability of the HMM.
                size = {n_states}

    init:       1D array-like
                The initial probability of HMM.
                size = {n_states}

    Returns
    -------
    float: Probability value for the obs to occur.
    """
    n_states = transition.shape[0]
    fwd = [{}]

    for i in range(n_states):
        fwd[0][y] = init[i] * emission[obs[0]]
    for t in range(1, len(obs)):
        fwd.append({})
        for i in range(n_states):
            fwd[t][i] = sum((fwd[t-1][y0] * transition[y0][i] *
emission[obs[t]]) for y0 in
                                range(n_states))
    prob = sum((fwd[len(obs) - 1][s]) for s in range(n_states))
    return prob
```

We can try to compute the probability by running it over some observations, as follows:

```
>>> obs = [0, 0, 0, 0] # Staying in the same location
>>> forward(obs, transition_matrix, emission, init_prob)
0.97381776799999997

>>> obs = [0, 10, 8, 6] # Should be 0 because can't jump from state 0 to
10.
>>> forward(obs, transition_matrix, emission, init_prob)
0.0
```

Computing the conditional distribution of the hidden state given the observations

Using the forward algorithm, we have been able to compute the value of $P(Z_x, X)$, so we might be tempted to think that we will easily be able to compute the conditional distribution $P(Z_k, X)$ using the following product rule:

$$P(Z_k|X) = \frac{P(Z_k, X)}{P(X)}$$

Computing the distribution, $P(X)$ however, is computationally intractable, as we will see. We can express $P(Z_k, X)$ as follows:

$$P(Z_k, X) = \sum_{Z_{i|i=1...n, i \neq k}} P(X, Z)$$

And hence we can compute $P(X)$ as the following:

$$P(X) = \sum_{Z_{1:n}} P(X, Z)$$
$$= \sum_{Z_1} \sum_{Z_2} \cdots \sum_{Z_n} P(X, Z)$$

If we look at the computational complexity of computing $P(X)$ using the preceding equation, it is $O(m^n)$, which is intractable for any sufficiently large value of m and n. And hence it is impossible to compute the conditional distribution of our hidden state using just the forward algorithm. In the next sections, we will introduce the backward algorithm and then we will show you how can we compute these conditional distributions.

Backward algorithm

Let's formally define the problem statement for the backward algorithm. In this case, we are trying to compute the probability of observation variables given the current state:

Backward algorithm: $P(X_{k+1:n} | Z_k)$

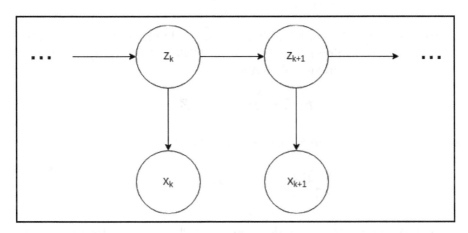

Figure 3.4: HMM showing two time slices, *k* and *k+1*

Similar to what we did in the case of the forward algorithm, we will again try to convert this probability term into a recursive equation in terms of known distributions, so that we can recursively compute the probabilities at different time instances. First, we introduce a new term, Z_{k+1} in $P(X_{k+1:n} | Z_k)$, using the marginalization rule:

$$P(X_{k+1:n}|Z_k) = \sum_{Z_{k+1}} P(X_{k+1:n}, Z_{k+1}|Z_k)$$

Here, we are marginalizing over the Z_{k+1} variable by summing over all of its possible states, which we have assumed to be *m*. Now, we can use the product rule of probability to split the preceding equation as:

$$P(X_{k+1:n}|Z_k) = \sum_{Z_{k+1}} P(X_{k+2:n}|Z_{k+1}, Z_k, X_{k+1})P(X_{k+1}|Z_{k+1}, Z_k)P(Z_{k+1}|Z_k)$$

Now, from the d-separation property of our model, we know that $X_{k+2:n} \perp Z_k, X_{k+1}|Z_{k+1}$. Also, we know from the definition of HMMs that $X_{k+1} \perp Z_k|Z_{k+1}$. Using these independent conditions, we can write our equation as:

$$P(X_{k+1:n}|Z_k) = \sum_{Z_{k+1}} P(X_{k+2:n}|Z_{k+1})P(X_{k+1}|Z_{k+1})P(Z_{k+1}|Z_k)$$

Now, the terms in our equation look familiar. The second term is the emission probability and the last term is the transition probability of our HMM. Now, to express it as a recursion, let's define a new function, β, given as:

$$\beta(k) = P(X_{k+1:n}|Z_k)$$

We can use β in the previous equation to represent it as a recursion:

$$\beta(k) = \sum_{Z_{k+1}} \beta(k+1)P(X_{k+1}|Z_{k+1})P(Z_{k+1}|Z_k)$$

Now, since we have the recursive equation, we can start computing the different values of β_k. But for computing the values, we will need to know at least one term of the recursion, so let's compute the value of $\beta(1)$:

$$\beta(1) = 1$$

```
def backward(obs, transition, emission, init):
    """
    Runs backward algorithm on the HMM.

    Parameters
    ----------
    obs:           1D list, array-like
                   The list of observed states.

    transition:    2D array-like
                   The transition probability of the HMM.
                   size = {n_states x n_states}

    emission:      1D array-like
                   The emission probabilitiy of the HMM.
                   size = {n_states}

    init:          1D array-like
```

```
                The initial probability of HMM.
                size = {n_states}

        Returns
        -------
        float: Probability value for the obs to occur.
        """
        n_states = transition.shape[0]
        bkw = [{} for t in range(len(obs))]
        T = len(obs)
        for y in range(n_states):
            bkw[T-1][y] = 1
        for t in reversed(range(T-1)):
            for y in range(n_states):
                bkw[t][y] = sum((bkw[t+1][y1] * transition[y][y1] *
emission[obs[t+1]]) for y1 in
                                        range(n_states))
        prob = sum((init[y] * emission[obs[0]] * bkw[0][y]) for y in
range(n_states))
        return prob
```

We can run this algorithm also on the same observations to see whether the results were correct:

```
>>> obs = [0, 0, 0, 0] # Staying in the same location
>>> backward(obs, transition_matrix, emission, init_prob)
0.97381776799999997

>>> obs = [0, 10, 8, 6] # Should be 0 because can't jump from state 0 to
10.
>>> backward(obs, transition_matrix, emission, init_prob)
0.0
```

Forward-backward algorithm (smoothing)

Coming to the forward-backward algorithm, we are now trying to compute the conditional distribution of the hidden state given the observations.

Taking the example of our robot localization, we are trying to now find the probability distribution of the robot's position at some time instance given the sensor readings:

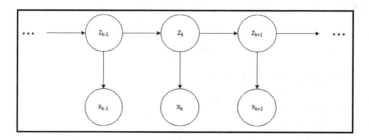

Forward-backward algorithm: $P(Z_k|X)$

Figure 3.5: HMM showing three time slices, $k-1$, k, and $k+1$

Now, since we have been given all the observed variables in the model, we can say that the value of $P(Z_k|X)$ is going to be proportional to the joint distribution over Z_k and X:

$$P(Z_k|X) \propto P(Z_k, X)$$

Now, we know that we can write $X=\{X_{1:k}, X_{k+1:n}\}$. Replacing this in the preceding equation, we get:

$$P(Z_k|X) \propto P(Z_k, X_{1:k}, X_{k+1:n})$$

We can apply the chain rule in the preceding equation to write it as:

$$P(Z_k|X) \propto P(X_{k+1:n}|Z_k, X_{1:k})P(Z_k, X_{1:k})$$

From our model structure, we know that $X_{k+1:n} \perp X_{1:k}|Z_k$, and using this independence property we can write the preceding equation as:

$$P(Z_k|X) \propto P(X_{k+1:n}|Z_k)P(Z_k, X_{1:k})$$

Now if we look at the preceding terms, the first term is $P(X_{k+1:n}|Z_k)$, which is what we computed in our backward algorithm. The second term is $P(Z_k, X_{1:k})$, which we computed in the case of the forward algorithm. So for computing $P(Z_k|X)$, we can compute both the terms using the forward and the backward algorithm. But since $P(Z_k|X)$ is proportional to the product of these two terms, we will need to normalize the distribution.

The Viterbi algorithm

So far, we have been trying to compute the different conditional and joint probabilities in our model. But one thing that we can't do with the forward-backward algorithm is find the most probable state of the hidden variables in the model given the observations. Formally, we can write this problem as, we know the observed variable, the transition probabilities and the emission probability of the network and we would like to compute Z^*, which is defined as:

$$Z^* = \underset{\mathbf{Z}}{\mathrm{argmax}}\, P(\mathbf{Z}|\mathbf{X})$$

Where,

$$Z=\{Z_1, Z_2, ..., Z_n\}$$

And,

$$X=\{X_1, X_2, ..., X_n\}$$

Properties of operations on probability distributions:
When we do operations on the probability distributions (marginalization, maximization, and so on), we can push in the operation through the independent terms of the distribution. We can see these examples in the case of marginalization and *argmax*:

$$\sum_X P(X, Z)P(Y) = P(Y)\sum_X P(X, Z)$$
$$\underset{X}{\mathrm{argmax}}\, P(X, Z)P(Y) = P(Y)\underset{X}{\mathrm{argmax}}\, P(X, Z)$$

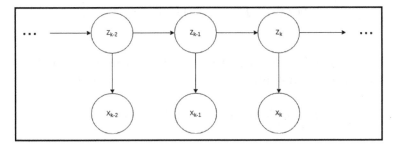

Figure 3.6: HMM showing three time slices *k-2*, *k-1*, and *k*

Since we saw that $P(Z|X) \propto P(Z, X)$, and since we are trying to compute the *argmax*, it wouldn't matter if we compute on either of these two terms. And hence we can say that:

$$\arg\max_{\mathbf{Z}} P(\mathbf{Z}|\mathbf{X}) = \arg\max_{\mathbf{Z}} P(\mathbf{Z}, \mathbf{X})$$

Now, we will again try to formulate our equation as a recursion so that it is easier for us to compute. So, let's introduce a new term, $\mu(k)$, defined as:

$$\mu(k) = \arg\max_{Z_{1:k-1}} P(Z_{1:k}, X_{1:k})$$

And again, we will try to break this term into known terms. Using the chain rule, we can write it as:

$$\mu(k) = \arg\max_{Z_{1:k-1}} P(X_k|Z_k)P(Z_k|Z_{k-1})P(Z_{1:k-1}, X_{1:k-1})$$

Now, we start pushing in the *argmax* argument using the property (see information box for details). And this gives us:

$$\mu(k) = \arg\max_{Z_{k-1}} \left[P(X_k|Z_k)P(Z_k|Z_{k-1}) \arg\max_{Z_{1:k-2}} P(Z_{1:k-1}, X_{1:k-1}) \right]$$

These terms look familiar, $P(X_k|Z_k)$ is the emission probability, $P(Z_k|Z_{k-1})$ is the transition probability, and $argmax_{Z_{1:k-2}} P(Z_{1:k-1}, X_{1:k-1})$ is $\mu(k-1)$. So now we have a recursive equation to work with:

$$\mu(k) = \arg\max_{Z_{k-1}} P(X_k|Z_k)P(Z_k|Z_{k-1})\mu(k-1)$$

Since we have the recursive formula, we can compute the values for any k if we have the first term. So, let's look at the first term of the recursion, which is $\mu(1)$:

$$\mu_1 = P(Z_1, X_1) = P(Z_1)P(X_1|Z_1)$$

Here, the first term is $P(Z_1)$, which is our initial probability, which is known. The second term is $P(X_1 | Z_1)$, which is the emission probability of our model:

```python
import numpy as np

def viterbi(obs, transition, emission, init=None):
    """
    Return the MAP estimate of state trajectory of Hidden Markov Model.

    Parameters
    ----------
    y : array (T,)
        Observation state sequence. int dtype.

    transition : array (K, K)
        State transition matrix. See HiddenMarkovModel.state_transition for
        details.

    emission : array (K,)
        Emission matrix. See HiddenMarkovModel.emission for details.

    init: optional, (K,)
        Initial state probabilities: Pi[i] is the probability x[0] == i. If
        None, uniform initial distribution is assumed (Pi[:] == 1/K).

    Returns
    -------
    x : array (T,)
        Maximum a posteriori probability estimate of hidden state
trajectory,
        conditioned on observation sequence y under the model parameters.

    T1: array (K, T)
        the probability of the most likely path so far

    T2: array (K, T)
        the x_j-1 of the most likely path so far
    """
    # Cardinality of the state space
    K = transition.shape[0]

    emission = np.repeat(emission[np.newaxis, :], K, axis=0)

    # Initialize the priors with default (uniform dist) if not given by
caller
    init = init if init is not None else np.full(K, 1 / K)
    T = len(obs)
    T1 = np.empty((K, T), 'd')
```

```
    T2 = np.empty((K, T), 'B')

    # Initilaize the tracking tables from first observation
    T1[:, 0] = init * emission[:, obs[0]]
    T2[:, 0] = 0

    # Iterate throught the observations updating the tracking tables
    for i in range(1, T):
        T1[:, i] = np.max(T1[:, i - 1] * transition.T *
emission[np.newaxis, :, obs[i]].T, 1)
        T2[:, i] = np.argmax(T1[:, i - 1] * transition.T, 1)

    # Build the output, optimal model trajectory
    x = np.empty(T, 'B')
    x[-1] = np.argmax(T1[:, T - 1])
    for i in reversed(range(1, T)):
        x[i - 1] = T2[x[i], i]

    return x, T1, T2
```

We can try it out with the same observations:

```
>>> x, T1, T2 = viterbi([0, 0, 0, 0], transition_matrix, emission,
init_prob)
>>> print(x)
array([0, 0, 0, 0], dtype=uint8)
>>> print(T1)
array([[ 0.077, 0.02541, 0.0083853, 0.00276715],
       [ 0.077, 0.02541, 0.0083853, 0.00276715],
       [ 0.077, 0.02541, 0.0083853, 0.00276715],
       [ 0.077, 0.02541, 0.0083853, 0.00276715],
       [ 0.077, 0.02541, 0.0083853, 0.00276715],
       [ 0.077, 0.02541, 0.0083853, 0.00276715],
       [ 0.077, 0.02541, 0.0083853, 0.00276715],
       [ 0.077, 0.02541, 0.0083853, 0.00276715],
       [ 0.077, 0.02541, 0.0083853, 0.00276715],
       [ 0.077, 0.02541, 0.0083853, 0.00276715],
       [ 0.077, 0.02541, 0.0083853, 0.00276715],
       [ 0.077, 0.02541, 0.0083853, 0.00276715],
       [ 0.077, 0.02541, 0.0083853, 0.00276715]])
>>> print(T2)
array([[ 0, 0, 0, 0],
       [ 0, 0, 0, 0],
       [ 0, 1, 1, 1],
       [ 0, 3, 3, 3],
       [ 0, 3, 3, 3],
       [ 0, 0, 0, 0],
       [ 0, 6, 6, 6],
```

```
       [ 0,  4,  4,  4],
       [ 0,  5,  5,  5],
       [ 0,  8,  8,  8],
       [ 0,  6,  6,  6],
       [ 0, 10, 10, 10],
       [ 0,  7,  7,  7]], dtype=uint8)

>>> x, T1, T2 = viterbi([0, 10, 8, 6], transition_matrix, emission,
init_prob)
>>> print(x)
array([0, 0, 0, 0], dtype=uint8)
>>> print(T1)
array([[ 0.077, 0., 0., 0. ],
       [ 0.077, 0., 0., 0. ],
       [ 0.077, 0., 0., 0. ],
       [ 0.077, 0., 0., 0. ],
       [ 0.077, 0., 0., 0. ],
       [ 0.077, 0., 0., 0. ],
       [ 0.077, 0., 0., 0. ],
       [ 0.077, 0., 0., 0. ],
       [ 0.077, 0., 0., 0. ],
       [ 0.077, 0., 0., 0. ],
       [ 0.077, 0., 0., 0. ],
       [ 0.077, 0., 0., 0. ],
       [ 0.077, 0., 0., 0. ]])

>>> print(T2)
array([[ 0,  0, 0, 0],
       [ 0,  0, 0, 0],
       [ 0,  1, 0, 0],
       [ 0,  3, 0, 0],
       [ 0,  3, 0, 0],
       [ 0,  0, 0, 0],
       [ 0,  6, 0, 0],
       [ 0,  4, 0, 0],
       [ 0,  5, 0, 0],
       [ 0,  8, 0, 0],
       [ 0,  6, 0, 0],
       [ 0, 10, 0, 0],
       [ 0,  7, 0, 0]], dtype=uint8)
```

Summary

In this chapter, we introduced algorithms for doing inference over our HMM models. We looked at the forward-backward algorithm to do predictions for our hidden states given the observations. We also discussed the Viterbi algorithm, which is used to compute the most probable states in our model.

In all these algorithms, we assumed that we knew the transition and the emission probabilities of the model. But in real-world problems, we need to compute these values from the data. In the next chapter, we will introduce algorithms for computing transition and emission probabilities using the maximum-likelihood approach.

4
Parameter Learning Using Maximum Likelihood

In the previous chapter, we discussed the state inference in the case of a **Hidden Markov Model** (**HMM**). We tried to predict the next state for an HMM using the information of previous state transitions. But in each cases, we had assumed that we already knew the transition and emission probabilities of the model. But in real-life problems, we usually need to learn these parameters from our observations.

In this chapter, we will try to estimate the parameters of our HMM model through data gathered from observations. We will be covering the following topics:

- Maximum likelihood learning, with examples
- Maximum likelihood learning in HMMs
- Expectation maximization algorithms
- The Baum-Welch algorithm

Maximum likelihood learning

Before diving into learning about **maximum likelihood estimation** (**MLE**) in HMMs, let's try to understand the basic concepts of MLE in generic cases. As the name suggests, MLE tries to select the parameters of the model that maximizes the likelihood of observed data. The likelihood for any model with given parameters is defined as the probability of getting the observed data, and can be written as follows:

$$\text{Likelihood: } P(D|\theta)$$

Here, $D=\{D_1, D_2, D_3, \ldots, D_n\}$ is the observed data, and θ is the set of parameters governing our model. In most cases, for simplicity, we assume that the datapoints are **independent and identically distributed** (**IID**). With that assumption, we can simplify the definition of our likelihood function as follows:

$$
\begin{aligned}
P(D|\theta) &= P(\{D_1, D_2, \ldots, D_n\}|\theta)\\
&= P(D_1|\theta)P(D_2|\theta)\ldots P(D_n|\theta)\\
&= \prod_{i=1}^{n} P(D_i|\theta)
\end{aligned}
$$

Here, we have used the multiplication rule for independent random variables to decompose the joint distribution into product over individual datapoint.

Coming back to MLE, MLE tries to find the value of θ for which the value of $P(D|\theta)$ is at a maximum. So, basically we now have an optimization problem at hand:

$$
\theta_{MLE} = \arg\max_{\theta} P(D|\theta)
$$

In the next couple of subsections, we will try to apply MLE to some simple examples to understand it better.

MLE in a coin toss

Let's assume that we want to learn a model of a given coin using observations obtained from tossing it. Since a coin can only have two outcomes, heads or tails, it can be modeled using a single parameter. Let's say we define the parameter as θ, which is the probability of getting heads when the coin is tossed. The probability of getting tails will automatically be $1-\theta$ because getting either heads or tails are mutually exclusive events.

We have our model ready, so let's move on to computing the likelihood function of this model. Let's assume that we are given some observations of coin tosses as $D=\{H,H,T,H,T,T\}$. For the given data we can write our likelihood function as follows:

$$
\begin{aligned}
P(D|\theta) &= P(\{H, H, T, H, T, T\}|\theta)\\
&= P(H|\theta)P(H|\theta)P(T|\theta)P(H|\theta)P(T|\theta)P(T|\theta)\\
&= \theta.\theta.(1-\theta).\theta.(1-\theta).(1-\theta)\\
&= \theta^3.(1-\theta)^3
\end{aligned}
$$

Now, we would like to find the value of θ that would maximize $P(D|\theta)$. For that, we take the derivative of our likelihood function, equate it to 0, and then solve it for θ:

$$\frac{\partial P(D|\theta)}{\partial \theta} = 0$$
$$3.\theta_{MLE}^2 (1 - \theta_{MLE})^3 - \theta_{MLE}^3 \cdot 3(1 - \theta_{MLE})^2 = 0$$
$$(1 - \theta_{MLE}) - \theta_{MLE} = 0$$
$$\theta_{MLE} = 0.5$$

Therefore, our MLE estimator learned that the probability of getting heads on tossing the coin is 0.5. Looking at our observations, we would expect the same probability as we have an equal number of heads and tails in our observed data.

Let's now try to write code to learn the parameter θ for our model. But as we know that finding the optimal value can run into numerical issues on a computer, is there a possible way to avoid that and directly be able to compute θ_{MLE}? If we look closely at our likelihood equation, we realize that we can write a generic formula for the likelihood for this model. If we assume that our data has n heads and m tails, we can write the likelihood as follows:

$$P(D|\theta) = \theta^n (1 - \theta)^m$$

Now, we can actually find θ_{MLE} in a closed-form using this likelihood function and avoid relying on any numerical method to compute the optimum value:

$$P(D|\theta) = \theta^n (1 - \theta)^m$$
$$\frac{\partial P(D|\theta)}{\partial \theta} = n\theta^{n-1}(1 - \theta)^m - m\theta^n (1 - \theta)^{(m-1)}$$
$$0 = n(1 - \theta_{MLE}) - m\theta_{MLE}$$
$$\theta_{MLE} = \frac{n}{n + m}$$

We can see that we have been able to find a closed form solution for the MLE solution to θ. Now, coding this up would be to simply compute the preceding formula as follows:

```python
import numpy as np


def coin_mle(data):
    """
    Returns the learned probability of getting a heads using MLE.
    Parameters
    ----------
    data: list, array-like
```

```
       The list of observations. 1 for heads and 0 for tails.
    Returns
    -------
    theta: The learned probability of getting a heads.
    """
    data = np.array(data)
    n_heads = np.sum(data)

    return n_heads / data.size
```

Now, let's try out our function for different datapoints:

```
>>> coin_mle([1, 1, 1, 0, 0])
0.59999999999999998

>>> coin_mle([1, 1, 1, 0, 0, 0])
0.5

>>> coin_mle([1, 1, 1, 0, 0, 0, 0])
0.42857142857142855
```

The outputs are as we expect, but one of the drawbacks of the MLE approach is that it is very sensitive to randomness in our data which, in some cases, might lead it to learn the wrong parameters. This is especially true in a case when the dataset is small in size. For example, let's say that we toss a fair coin three times and we get heads in each toss. The MLE approach, in this case, would learn the value of θ to be 1, which is not correct since we had a fair coin. The output is as follows:

```
>>> coin_mle([1, 1, 1])
1.0
```

In Chapter 5, *Parameter Inference using Bayesian Approach*, we will try to solve this problem of MLE by starting with a prior distribution over the parameters, and it modifies its prior as it sees more and more data.

MLE for normal distributions

In the previous section, we had a model with a single parameter. In this section, we will apply the same concepts to a slightly more complex model. We will try to learn the parameters of a normal distribution (also known as the **Gaussian distribution**) from a given observed data. As we know, the normal distribution is parametrized by its mean and standard deviation and the distribution is given as follows:

$$P(x|\mu, \sigma) = \frac{1}{\sqrt{2\pi\sigma^2}} \exp^{-\frac{(x-\mu)^2}{2\sigma^2}}$$

Here, μ is the mean and σ is the standard deviation of the normal distribution.

As we discussed earlier, for estimating parameters using MLE we would need some observed data, which, in this case, we are assuming to be coming from a normal distribution (or that it can be approximated using a normal distribution). Let's assume that we have some observed data: $X = \{x_1, x_2,...,x_N\}$. We want to estimate the parameters μ (mean) and σ^2 (variance) for our model.

We will follow the same steps as we took in the previous section. We will start by defining the likelihood function for the normal distribution. The likelihood is the probability of the data being observed, given the parameters. So, given the observed data, we can state the likelihood function as follows:

$$\begin{aligned}
\mathbf{L}(\mu, \sigma^2) &= Pr(X|\mu, \sigma^2) \\
&= Pr(x_1, \ldots, x_N|\mu, \sigma^2) \\
&= \prod_{n=1}^{N} Pr(x_n|\mu, \sigma^2) \\
&= \prod_{n=1}^{N} \frac{1}{\sqrt{2\pi}\sigma} \exp\left\{\frac{-(x_n - \mu)^2}{2\sigma^2}\right\}
\end{aligned}$$

One issue that we usually run into while trying to work with the product of small numbers is that the number can get too small for the computer to work with. To avoid running into this issue, we instead work with the log-likelihood instead of the simple likelihood. Since log is an increasing function, the maximum of the log-likelihood function would be for the same value of parameters as it would have been for the likelihood function. The log-likelihood can be defined as follows:

$$\begin{aligned}
\log L(\mu, \sigma^2) &= \log\left[\prod_{n=1}^{N} \frac{1}{\sqrt{2\pi\sigma^2}} \exp^{-\frac{(x_n-\mu)^2}{2\sigma^2}}\right] \\
\mathcal{L}(\mu, \sigma^2) &= \sum_{n=1}^{N}\left[\log \frac{1}{\sqrt{2\pi\sigma^2}} - \frac{(x_n - \mu)^2}{2\sigma^2}\right] \\
\mathcal{L}(\mu, \sigma^2) &= -\frac{N}{2}\log(2\pi\sigma^2) - \sum_{n=1}^{N} \frac{(x_n - \mu)^2}{2\sigma^2}
\end{aligned}$$

We can then find the values of μ_{MLE} and σ_{MLE} that maximize the log-likelihood function by taking partial derivatives with respect to each of the variables, equating it to 0, and solving the equation. To get the mean value, we need to take the partial derivative of the log-likelihood function with respect to μ while keeping σ as constant, and set it to 0, which gives us the following:

$$\sum_{n=1}^{N}(x_n - \mu_{MLE}) = 0$$

$$\mu_{MLE} = \frac{1}{N}\sum_{n=1}^{N}x_n$$

Similarly, the MLE of standard deviation σ^2 can be computed by the partial derivative of the log-likelihood function with σ^2 while keeping μ constant, equating it to 0, and then solving for σ^2:

$$\sigma_{MLE}^2 = \frac{1}{N}\sum_{n=1}^{N}(x_n - \mu_{MLE})^2$$

As we can see, we have again been able to derive a closed-form solution for the MLE and thus wouldn't need to rely on numerical methods while coding it up. Let's try to code this up and check if our MLE approach has learnt the correct parameters:

```python
import numpy as np


def gaussian_mle(data):
    """
    Returns the learned parameters of the Normal Distribution using MLE.

    Parameters
    ----------
    data: list, array-like
    The list of observed variables.

    Returns
    -------
    \mu: The learned mean of the Normal Distribution.
    \sigma: The learned standard deviation of the Normal Distribution.
    """
    data = np.array(data)
```

```
mu = np.mean(data)
variance = np.sqrt(np.mean((data - mu)**2))

return mu, variance
```

We have our learning function ready, so we can now generate some data from a known distribution and check if our function is able to learn the same parameters from the generated data:

```
>>> from numpy.random import normal
>>> data = normal(loc=1, scale=2, size=10)
>>> data
array([ 1.8120102, 2.14363679, 1.49010868, -1.95531206, 1.62449155,
        1.49345327, 1.48957918, -0.67536313, 4.31506202, 4.24883442])

>>> mu, sigma = gaussian_mle(data)
>>> mu
1.5986500906187573
>>> sigma
1.805051208889392
```

In this example, we can see that the learned values are not very accurate. This is because of the problem with the MLE being too sensitive to the observed datapoints, as we discussed in the previous section. Let's try to run this same example with more observed data:

```
>>> data = normal(loc=1, scale=2, size=1000)
>>> data[:10]
array([ 4.5855015, 1.55162883, -1.61385859, 0.52543984, 0.90247428,
        3.40717092, 1.4078157, 0.01560836, -1.19409859, -0.01641439])

>>> mu, sigma = gaussian_mle(data)
>>> mu
 1.0437186891666821
>>> sigma
1.967211026428509
```

In this case, with more data, we can see that the learned values are much closer to our original values.

MLE for HMMs

Having a basic understanding of MLE, we can now move on to applying these concepts to the case of HMMs. In the next few subsections, we will see two possible scenarios of learning in HMMs, namely, supervised learning and unsupervised learning.

Supervised learning

In the case of supervised learning, we use the data generated by sampling the process that we are trying to model. If we are trying to parameterize our HMM model using simple discrete distributions, we can simply apply the MLE to compute the transition and emission distributions by counting the number of transitions from any given state to another state. Similarly, we can compute the emission distribution by counting the output states from different hidden states. Therefore the transition and emission probabilities can be computed as follows:

$$t(i, j) = \# \text{ of } i \rightarrow j \text{ transitions in data}$$
$$e(i, s) = \# \text{ of emissions of type } s \text{ at state } i$$
$$T(i, j) = \frac{t(i, j)}{\sum_k t(i, k)}$$
$$E(i, s) = \frac{e(i, s)}{\sum_{S'} e(i, S')}$$

Here, *T(i,j)* is the transition probability from state *i* to state *j*. And *E(i,s)* is the emission probability of getting state *s* from state *i*.

Let's take a very simple example to make this clearer. We want to model the weather and whether or not it would rain over a period of time. Also, we assume that the weather can take three possible states:

- *Sunny (S)*
- *Cloudy (C)*
- *Windy (W)*

And the *Rain* variable can have two possible states; *that it rained (R)* or *that it didn't rain (NR)*. An HMM model would look something like this:

And let's say we have some observed data for this which looks something like D={(S,NR), (S,NR), (C,NR), (C,R), (C,R), (W,NR), (S,NR), (W,R), (C,NR)}. Here, the first element of each datapoint represents the observed weather that day and the second element represents whether it rained or not that day. Now, using the formulas that we derived earlier, we can easily compute the transition and emission probabilities. We will start with computing the transition probability from *S* to *S*:

$$t(S, S) = 1$$
$$\sum_{k} t(i, k) = t(S, S) + t(S, C) + t(S, R) = 1 + 1 + 1 = 3$$
$$T(S, S) = 1/3$$

Similarly, we can compute the transition probabilities for all the other combinations of states:

$$T(S, C) = 1/3$$
$$T(S, R) = 1/3$$
$$T(C, S) = 0$$
$$T(C, C) = 2/3$$
$$T(C, W) = 1/3$$
$$T(W, S) = 1/2$$
$$T(W, C) = 1/2$$
$$T(W, W) = 0$$

And, hence, we have our complete transition probability over all the possible states of the weather. We can represent it in tabular form to look nicer:

	Sunny(S)	Cloudy(C)	Windy(W)
Sunny(S)	0.33	0.33	0.33
Cloudy(C)	0	0.66	0.33
Windy(W)	0.5	0.5	0

Table 1: Transition probability for the weather model

Now, coming to computing the emission probability, we can again just follow the formula derived previously:

$$e(W, R) = 1$$
$$\sum_{S'} e(W, S') = e(W, R) + e(W, NR) = 1 + 1 = 2$$
$$E(W, R) = 1/2$$

Similarly, we can compute all the other values in the distribution:

$$E(W, NR) = 1/2$$
$$E(S, R) = 0$$
$$E(S, NR) = 1$$
$$E(C, R) = 1/2$$
$$E(C, NR) = 1/2$$

And hence our emission probability can be written in tabular form as follows:

	Sunny(S)	Cloudy(C)	Windy(W)
Rain (R)	0	0.5	0.5
No Rain (NR)	1	0.5	0.5

Table 2: Emission probability for the weather model

In the previous example, we saw how we can compute the parameters of an HMM using MLE and some simple computations. But, because in this case we had assumed the transition and emission probabilities as simple discrete conditional distribution, the computation was much easier. With more complex cases, we will need to estimate more parameters than we did in the previous section in the case of the normal distribution.

Code

Let's now try to code up the preceding algorithm:

```
def weather_fit(data):
    """
    Learn the transition and emission probabilities from the given data
    for the weather model.

    Parameters
    ----------
    data: 2-D list (array-like)
    Each data point should be a tuple of size 2 with the first element
    representing the state of Weather and the second element representing
    whether it rained or not.
    Sunny = 0, Cloudy = 1, Windy = 2
    Rain = 0, No Rain = 1

    Returns
    -------
    transition probability: 2-D array
```

```
The conditional distribution representing the transition probability
of the model.
emission probability: 2-D array
The conditional distribution representing the emission probability
of the model.
"""

data = np.array(data)

transition_counts = np.zeros((3, 3))
emission_counts = np.zeros((3, 2))

for index, datapoint in enumerate(data):
    if index != len(data)-1:
        transition_counts[data[index][0], data[index+1][0]] += 1
    emission_counts[data[index][0], data[index][1]] += 1

transition_prob = transition_counts / np.sum(transition_counts, axis=0)
emission_prob = (emission_counts.T / np.sum(emission_counts.T,
axis=0)).T

return transition_prob, emission_prob
```

Let's generate some data and try learning the parameters using the preceding function:

```
>>> import numpy as np
>>> weather_data = np.random.randint(low=0, high=3, size=1000)
>>> rain_data = np.random.randint(low=0, high=2, size=1000)
>>> data = list(zip(weather_data, rain_data))
>>> transition_prob, emission_prob = weather_fit(data)
>>> transition_prob
array([[ 0.3125, 0.38235294, 0.27272727],
       [ 0.28125, 0.38235294, 0.36363636],
       [ 0.40625, 0.23529412, 0.36363636]])

>>> emission_prob
array([[ 0.3125, 0.38235294, 0.27272727],
       [ 0.28125, 0.38235294, 0.36363636],
       [ 0.40625, 0.23529412, 0.36363636]])
```

Unsupervised learning

In the previous section, we saw how we can use supervised learning in a case where we have all the variables observed, including the hidden variables. But that is usually not the case with real-life problems. For such cases, we use unsupervised learning to estimate the parameters of the model.

The two main learning algorithms used for this are the following:

- The Viterbi learning algorithm
- The Baum-Welch algorithm

We will discuss these in the next couple of subsections.

Viterbi learning algorithm

The Viterbi learning algorithm (not to be confused with the Viterbi algorithm for state estimation) takes a set of training observations O^r, with $1 \leq r \leq R$, and estimates the parameters of a single HMM by iteratively computing Viterbi alignments. When used to initialize a new HMM, the Viterbi segmentation is replaced by a uniform segmentation (that is, each training observation is divided into N equal segments) for the first iteration.

Other than the first iteration on a new model, each training sequence O is segmented using a state alignment procedure which results from maximizing:

$$\phi_N(T) = \max_i \phi_i(T) a_i N$$

for *1<i<N* where:

$$\phi_j(t) = \left[\max_i \phi_i(t-1) a_{ij} \right] b_j(O_t)$$

And the initial conditions are given by:

$$\phi_1(1) = 1$$

$$\phi_j(1) = a_{1j} b_j(O_1)$$

for 1<*j*<*N*. And, in the discrete case, the output probability $b_j(.)$ is defined as:

$$b_j(O_t) = \prod_{s=1}^{S} \{P_{js}[v_s(O_{st})]\}^{\gamma_s}$$

where S is the total number of streams, $v_s(O_{st})$ is the output given, the input $O_{st,}$ and $P_{js}[v]$ is the probability of state j to give an output v.

If A_{ij} represents the total number of transitions from state i to state j in performing the preceding maximizations, then the transition probabilities can be estimated from the relative frequencies:

$$\hat{a}_{ij} = \frac{A_{ij}}{\sum_{k=2}^{N} A_{ik}}$$

The sequence of states that maximizes $\varnothing_N(T)$ implies an alignment of training data observations with states. Within each state, a further alignment of observations to mixture components is made. Usually, two mechanisms can be used for this, for each state and each output stream:

- Use clustering to allocate each observation O_{st} to one of M_s clusters
- Associate each observation O_{st} with the mixture component with the highest probability

In either case, the net result is that every observation is associated with a single unique mixture component. This association can be represented by the indicator $\psi_{jsm}^r(t)$ function , which is *1* if O_{st}^r is associated with a mixture component *m* of stream *s* of state *j*, and is zero otherwise.

The means and variances are then estimated by computing simple means:

$$\hat{\mu}_{jsm} = \sum_{r=1}^{R}\sum_{t=1}^{T_r} \psi_{jsm}^r O_{st}^r \sum_{r=1}^{R}\sum_{t=1}^{T_r} \psi_{jsm}^r(t)$$

$$\hat{\Sigma}_{jsm} = \sum_{r=1}^{R}\sum_{t=1}^{T} \psi_{jsm}^r(t)(O_{st}^r - \hat{\mu_{jsm}})' \sum_{r=1}^{R}\sum_{t=1}^{T_r} \psi_{jsm}^r(t)$$

And the mixture weights are based on the number of observations allocated to each component:

$$c_{jsm} = \sum_{r=1}^{R} \sum_{t=1}^{T_r} \sum_{l=1}^{M_s} \psi_{jsl}^r(t)$$

The Baum-Welch algorithm (expectation maximization)

The **expectation maximization** (**EM**) algorithm (known as **Baum-Welch** when applied to HMMs) is an iterative method used to find the maximum likelihood or **maximum a posteriori** (**MAP**) estimates of parameters in statistical models, where the model depends on unobserved latent variables. The EM iteration alternates between performing an **expectation** (**E**) step, which creates a function for the expectation of the log-likelihood evaluated using the current estimate for the parameters, and a **maximization** (**M**) step, which computes parameters maximizing the expected log-likelihood found on the *E* step. These parameter estimates are then used to determine the distribution of the latent variables in the next *E* step.

The EM algorithm starts with initial value of parameters (θ^{old}). In the *E* step, we take these parameters and find the posterior distribution of latent variables $P(Z|X,\theta^{old})$. We then use this posterior distribution to evaluate the expectation of the logarithm of the complete data likelihood function, as a function of the parameters θ, to give the function $Q(\theta,\theta^{old})$, defined by the following:

$$Q(\theta, \theta^{old}) = \sum_{\mathbf{Z}} Pr(\mathbf{Z}|\mathbf{X}, \theta^{old}) \ln Pr(\mathbf{X}, \mathbf{Z}|\theta)$$

Let's introduce some terms that can help us in the future. $\gamma(Z_n)$ to denote the marginal posterior distribution of a latent variable:

$$\gamma(z_n) = Pr(z_n|\mathbf{X}, \theta^{old})$$

$\xi(z_{n-1}, z_n)$ denoting the marginal posterior distribution of two successive latent variables:

$$\xi(z_{n-1}, z_n) = Pr(z_{n-1}, z_n|\mathbf{X}, \theta^{old})$$

Thus, for each value of n, we can store $\gamma(Z_n)$ as a vector of K non-negative numbers that sum to 1, and, similarly we can use a $K \times K$ matrix of non-negative numbers that sum to 1 to save $\xi(z_{n-1}, z_n)$.

As we have discussed in previous chapters, the latent variable z_n can be represented as K dimensional binary variable where $z_{nk} = 1$ when z_n is in state k. We can also use it to denote the conditional probability of $z_{nk} = 1$, and similarly $\xi(z_{n-1}, j, z_{nk})$ to denote the conditional probability of $zn\text{-}1, j = 1$, and $z_{nk} = 1$. As the expectation of a binary random variable is just the probability of its value being 1, we can state the following:

$$\gamma(z_{nk}) = \mathbb{E}[z_{nk}] = \sum_{\mathbf{z}} \gamma(\mathbf{z}) z_{nk}$$

$$\xi(z_{n-1,j}, z_{nk}) = \mathbb{E}[z_{n-1,j} z_{nk}] = \sum_{\mathbf{z}} \gamma(\mathbf{z}) z_{n-1,j} z_{nk}$$

As we discussed in the previous chapter, the joint probability distribution of an HMM can be represented as follows:

$$P(\mathbf{X}, \mathbf{Z}|\theta) = P(\mathbf{z}_1|\pi)\left[\prod_{n=2}^{N} P(\mathbf{z}_n|\mathbf{z}_{n-1}, \mathbf{A})\right] \prod_{m=2}^{N} P(\mathbf{x}_m|\mathbf{z}_m, \phi)$$

Thus we can write the data likelihood function as follows:

$$Q(\theta, \theta^{old}) = \sum_{k=1}^{K} \gamma(z_{1k}) \ln \pi_k + \sum_{n=2}^{N}\sum_{j=1}^{K}\sum_{i=1}^{K} \xi(z_{n-1,j}, z_{nk}) \ln A_{jk}$$

$$+ \sum_{n=2}^{N}\sum_{k=1}^{K} \gamma(z_{nk}) \ln Pr(\boldsymbol{x}_n|\phi_k)$$

In the E step we try to evaluate the quantities $\gamma(z_n)$ and $\xi(z_{n-1}, z_n)$ efficiently. For efficient computation of these two terms we can use either a forward backward algorithm or the Viterbi algorithm as discussed in the previous chapter. And in the M step, we try to maximize the value of $Q(\theta, \theta^{old})$ with respect to the parameters $\theta = \{A, \pi, \Phi\}$ in which we treat $\gamma(z_n)$ and $\xi(z_{n-1}, z_n)$ as constants.

In doing so, we get the MLE values of the parameters as follows:

$$\pi_k = \frac{\gamma(z_{1k})}{\sum_{j=1}^{K} \gamma(z_{1j})}$$

$$A_{jk} = \frac{\sum_{n=2}^{N} \xi(z_{n-1,j}, z_{nk})}{\sum_{l=1}^{K} \sum_{n=2}^{N} \xi(z_{n-1,j}, z_{nl})}$$

If we assume the emission distribution to be a normal distribution such that $Pr(\mathbf{x}|\phi_k) = \mathcal{N}(\mathbf{x}|\mu_k, \Sigma_k)$, then the maximization of $Q(\theta, \theta^{old})$ with respect to Φ_k would result in the following:

$$\mu_k = \frac{\sum_{n=1}^{N} \gamma(z_{nk})\mathbf{x}_n}{\sum_{n=1}^{N} \gamma(z_{nk})}$$

$$\Sigma_k = \frac{\sum_{n=1}^{N} \gamma(z_{nk})(\mathbf{x}_n - \mu_k)(\mathbf{x}_n - \mu_k)^{\mathrm{T}}}{\sum_{n=1}^{N} \gamma(z_{nk})}$$

The EM algorithm must be initialized by choosing starting values for π and A, which should, of course, be non-negative and should add up to 1.

Code

The algorithms for parameter estimation look quite complex but `hmmlearn`, a Python package for working with HMMs, has great implementations for it. `hmmlearn` is also hosted on PyPI so it can be installed directly using `pip`: `pip install hmmlearn`. For the code example, we will take an example of stock price prediction by learning a Gaussian HMM on stock prices. This example has been taken from the examples page of `hmmlearn`.

For the example, we also need the `matplotlib` and `datetime` packages which can also be installed using `pip`:

```
pip install matplotlib datetime
```

Coming to the code, we should start by importing all the required packages:

```
from __future__ import print_function

import datetime

import numpy as np
from matplotlib import cm, pyplot as plt
from matplotlib.dates import YearLocator, MonthLocator

try:
    from matplotlib.finance import quotes_historical_yahoo_ochl
except ImportError:
    # For Matplotlib prior to 1.5.
    from matplotlib.finance import (
        quotes_historical_yahoo as quotes_historical_yahoo_ochl
    )

from hmmlearn.hmm import GaussianHMM

print(__doc__)
```

Next, we will fetch our stock price data from Yahoo! Finance:

```
quotes = quotes_historical_yahoo_ochl(
    "INTC", datetime.date(1995, 1, 1), datetime.date(2012, 1, 6))

# Unpack quotes
dates = np.array([q[0] for q in quotes], dtype=int)
close_v = np.array([q[2] for q in quotes])
volume = np.array([q[5] for q in quotes])[1:]

# Take diff of close value. Note that this makes
# ``len(diff) = len(close_t) - 1``, therefore, other quantities also
# need to be shifted by 1.
diff = np.diff(close_v)
dates = dates[1:]
close_v = close_v[1:]

# Pack diff and volume for training.
X = np.column_stack([diff, volume])
```

Next, we define a Gaussian HMM model and learn the parameters for our data:

```
# Make an HMM instance and execute fit
model = GaussianHMM(n_components=4, covariance_type="diag",
n_iter=1000).fit(X)

# Predict the optimal sequence of internal hidden state
hidden_states = model.predict(X)
```

We can now print out our learned parameters:

```
print("Transition matrix")
print(model.transmat_)
print()

print("Means and vars of each hidden state")
for i in range(model.n_components):
    print("{0}th hidden state".format(i))
    print("mean = ", model.means_[i])
    print("var = ", np.diag(model.covars_[i]))
    print()
```

The output is as follows:

```
Transition matrix
[[  9.79220773e-01   2.57382344e-15   2.72061945e-03   1.80586073e-02]
 [  1.12216188e-12   7.73561269e-01   1.85019044e-01   4.14196869e-02]
 [  3.25313504e-03   1.12692615e-01   8.83368021e-01   6.86228435e-04]
 [  1.18741799e-01   4.20310643e-01   1.18670597e-18   4.60947557e-01]]

Means and vars of each hidden state
0th hidden state
mean =  [  2.33331888e-02   4.97389989e+07]
var =  [  6.97748259e-01   2.49466578e+14]

1st hidden state
mean =  [  2.12401671e-02   8.81882861e+07]
var =  [  1.18665023e-01   5.64418451e+14]

2nd hidden state
mean =  [  7.69658065e-03   5.43135922e+07]
var =  [  5.02315562e-02   1.54569357e+14]

3rd hidden state
mean =  [ -3.53210673e-01   1.53080943e+08]
var =  [  2.55544137e+00   5.88210257e+15]
```

We can also plot our hidden states over time:

```
fig, axs = plt.subplots(model.n_components, sharex=True, sharey=True)
colours = cm.rainbow(np.linspace(0, 1, model.n_components))
for i, (ax, colour) in enumerate(zip(axs, colours)):
    # Use fancy indexing to plot data in each state.
    mask = hidden_states == i
    ax.plot_date(dates[mask], close_v[mask], ".-", c=colour)
    ax.set_title("{0}th hidden state".format(i))

    # Format the ticks.
    ax.xaxis.set_major_locator(YearLocator())
    ax.xaxis.set_minor_locator(MonthLocator())

    ax.grid(True)

plt.show()
```

The output of the preceding code is as follows:

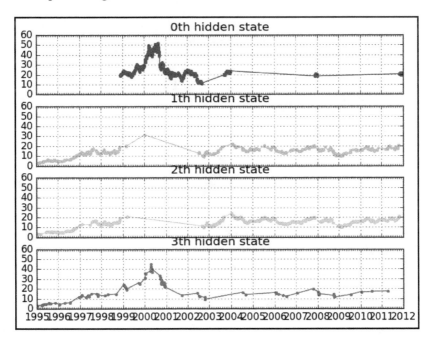

Figure 1: Plot of hidden states over time

Summary

In this chapter, we introduced algorithms for doing parameter estimation of a given HMM model. We started by looking into the basics of MLE and then applied the concepts to HMMs. For HMM training, we looked into two different scenarios: supervised training, when we have the observations for the hidden states, and unsupervised training, when we only have the output observations.

We also talked about the problems with estimation using MLE. In the next chapter, we will introduce algorithms for doing parameter estimation using the Bayesian approach, which tries to solve these issues.

Parameter Inference Using the Bayesian Approach

5

In the previous chapter, we discussed inferring the parameters using the maximum-likelihood approach. In this chapter, we will explore the same issue through a Bayesian approach. The main topics are as follows:

- Introduction to Bayesian learning
- Bayesian learning in HMMs
- Approximate algorithms for estimating distributions

Bayesian learning

In the maximum-likelihood approach to learning, we try to find the most optimal parameters for our model that maximizes our likelihood function. But data in real life is usually really noisy, and in most cases, it doesn't represent the true underlying distribution. In such cases, the maximum-likelihood approach fails. For example, consider tossing a fair coin a few times. It is possible that all of our tosses result in either heads or tails. If we use a maximum-likelihood approach on this data, it will assign a probability of 1 to either heads or tails, which would suggest that we would never get the other side of the coin. Or, let's take a less extreme case: let's say we toss a coin 10 times and get three heads and seven tails. In this case, a maximum-likelihood approach will assign a probability of 0.3 to heads and 0.7 to tails, which is not the true distribution of a fair coin. This problem is also commonly known as **overfitting**.

Bayesian learning takes a slightly different approach to learn these parameters. We start by assigning a prior distribution over the parameters of our model. The prior makes our assumptions about the model explicit. In the case of tossing the coin, we can start by using a prior that assigns equal probabilities to both heads and tails. Then we apply the Bayes theorem to compute the posterior distribution over our parameters based on the data. This allows us to shift our belief (prior) toward where the data points to, and this makes us do a less extreme estimate of the parameters. And in this way, Bayesian learning can solve one of the major drawbacks of maximum likelihood.

In more general terms, in the case of Bayesian learning, we try to learn a distribution over the parameters of our model instead of learning a single parameter that maximizes the likelihood. For learning this distribution over the parameters, we use the Bayes theorem, given by the following:

$$P(\theta|D) = \frac{P(D|\theta)P(\theta)}{P(D)}$$

Here, $P(\theta)$ is our prior over the parameters of the model, $P(D|\theta)$ is the likelihood of the data given the parameters, and $P(D)$ is the probability of the observed data. $P(D)$ can also be written in terms of prior and likelihood as follows:

$$P(D) = \sum_{\theta} P(D,\theta) = \sum_{\theta} P(D|\theta)P(\theta)$$

Now let's talk about each of these terms separately and see how can we compute them. The prior, $P(\theta)$, is a probability distribution over the parameters representing our belief about the values of the parameters. For example, in the case of coin tossing, we can have our initial belief as θ is in between 0 and 1 and is uniformly distributed. The likelihood term, $P(D|\theta)$, is the same term that we tried to maximize in Chapter 4, *Parameter Inference using Maximum Likelihood*. It represents how likely our observed data is, given the parameters of the model. The next term, $P(D)$, is the probability of observing our data and it acts as the normalizing term. It is computationally difficult to compute because it requires us to sum over all the possible values of θ and, for any sufficiently large number of parameters, it quickly becomes intractable. In the next sections of this chapter, we will see the different algorithms that we can use to approximate these values. The term that we are trying to compute, $P(D|\theta)$, is known as the **posterior**. It represents our final probability distribution over the parameters of the model given our observed data. Basically, our prior is updated using the likelihood term to give the final distribution.

Another problem that Bayesian learning solves is the model selection. Since Bayesian learning gives a distribution over the different possible models rather than a single model, we have a couple of options of how we want to do predictions from these models. The first method is to just select a specific model that has the maximum probability, which is also commonly known as the **Maximum Aposteriori** (**MAP**) estimate. The other possible way is to compute the expectation of the prediction from all the models based on the posterior distribution. This allows us to regularize our predictions since we are computing expectation over all possible models.

Selecting the priors

A common question when doing Bayesian learning is how to select the appropriate prior. As David Mackay has said, *there is no inference without assumptions, we need to make a guess for the prior*. Our prior should be representative of what we think the most likely parameters are for our model. A huge benefit of using our own prior is that we make our assumption about the model explicit. Once we start applying Bayes, theorem using our prior and the observed data, our posterior would be a shift from our prior toward a distribution that represents our data better.

Theoretically, this sounds good as we can probably select very complex priors that capture our idea of the model, but for applying the Bayes theorem, we need to multiply our prior with the likelihood, and for complex distributions, it very quickly becomes computationally intractable. Therefore, in practice, we usually select a prior that is a conjugate distribution to our likelihood. A conjugate prior allows us to have a closed-form solution to the Bayes theorem. Because of this, Gaussian distributions are used for priors and likelihoods as multiplying a Gaussian distribution with another Gaussian distribution results in a Gaussian distribution. Also computations it's not expensive to compute the product of two Gaussians.

Intractability

Apart from selecting difficult priors, another source of intractability in Bayesian learning is the denominator term of Bayes' theorem:

$$P(D) = \sum_{\theta} P(D, \theta) = \sum_{\theta} P(D|\theta)P(\theta)$$

As we can see in the preceding equation for computing *P(D)*, we need to compute a summation over all the possible values of θ, which is the set of all the parameters of our model. If we have a lot of parameters in our model, it is computationally intractable to compute this term since the size of the term grows exponentially with the number of parameters. A lot of work has been done to approximate this value, as we will see in the next section of this chapter.

Bayesian learning in HMM

As we saw in the previous section, in the case of Bayesian learning we assume all the variables as a random variable, assign a prior to it, and then try to compute the posterior based on that. Therefore, in the case of HMM, we can assign a prior on our transition probabilities, emission probabilities, or the number of observation states.

Therefore, the first problem that we need to solve is to select the prior. Theoretically, a prior can be any distribution over the parameters of the model, but in practice, we usually try to use a conjugate prior to the likelihood, so that we have a closed-form solution to the equation. For example, in the case when the output of the HMM is discrete, a common choice of prior is the Dirichlet distribution. It is mainly for two reasons, the first of which is that the Dirichlet distribution is a conjugate distribution to multinomial distribution which allows us to multiply them easily.

Conjugate distribution: A family of priors is said to be conjugate to a family of likelihoods if the posterior obtained by multiplying the prior by the likelihood is in the same family of distribution as the prior distribution.

For example, since the likelihood of the initial state given the π parameter vector is multinomial:

$$P(S_1|\pi) = \prod_{i=1}^{K} \pi_i^{S_{1i}}$$

And if the prior probability of π is Dirichlet:

$$P(\pi) = \frac{1}{Z} \prod_{i=1}^{K} \pi_i^{u_i - 1}$$

Where $u = [u_1, u_2, ..., u_K]$ is the hyperparameter vector and Z is the normalizing constant. We can now compute the posterior from the likelihood and the prior, which is given as follows:

$$P(\pi|S_1) = \frac{1}{Z'} \prod_{i=1}^{K} \pi_i^{u_i + S_{1i} - 1}$$

And we can see that the posterior is also a Dirichlet distribution. Hence we can say that the Dirichlet distribution is a conjugate prior to the multinomial distribution. And in a similar way, we can set up Dirichlet priors for our transition matrix and emission matrix.

The second reason for choosing a Dirichlet prior is that it has the desirable property that its hyperparameters can be interpreted as a hypothetical count of observations. In the preceding example, if $u_i = 2$ and $u_j = 1$ for $j \neq i$, the MAP estimate of π would be the same as a maximum-likelihood estimation with the assumption that the training data had an extra data point with the initial state being in state i. This conjugate property allows us to do MAP estimation in the case of Dirichlet priors by doing a minor variation in the Baum-Welch algorithm. It also gives theoretical justification for the seemingly ad hoc but very common regularization method for HMMs, which just adds a small positive number to all elements of the parameter vector.

In the last couple of paragraphs, we talked specifically about the case when the output is discrete. But the same concepts can be extended to the case of continuous output as well. Conjugate distributions exist in the case of continuous distributions as well. One of the most commonly used distributions is the Gaussian distribution as it stays in the same family after different operations.

Approximating required integrals

As we discussed before, the Bayesian approach treats all unknown quantities as random variables. We assign prior distributions to these variables and then estimate the posterior distribution over these after the data is observed. In the case of HMMs, the unknown quantities comprise the structure of the HMM, that is, the number of states, the parameters of the network, and the hidden states. Unlike maximum-likelihood or MAP estimations, in which we find point estimates for these parameters, we now have distributions over these parameters. This allows us to compare between model structures, but for doing that we need to integrate over both the parameters and the hidden states of the model. This is commonly known as Bayesian integration.

Since these integrations are computationally intractable, we resort to approximate methods to compute these values. In the next few subsections, we will give an overview of some of these methods. A detailed analysis of these methods is outside the scope of this book.

Sampling methods

Sampling methods are one of the most common ways to estimate intractable distributions. The general idea is to sample points from the distribution space in a way such that we get more samples from high-probability areas. And then based on these samples we estimate the distributions.

Laplace approximations

Laplace approximations use the central limit theorem, which from well-behaved priors and data asserts that the posterior parameter will converge in the limit of a large number of training samples to a Gaussian around the MAP estimate of the parameters. To estimate the evidence using the Laplace approximation, MAP parameters are found in the usual optimization routines and then the Hessian of the log-likelihood is computed at the MAP estimate. The evidence is approximated by evaluating the $P(\theta,D)/P(\theta|D)$ ratio at the MAP estimate of θ, using the Gaussian approximation in the denominator. The Laplace approximation suffers from several disadvantages:

- Computing the Hessian matrix from the parameters is usually very costly
- The Gaussian approximation is not very good for models with parameters that are positive and sum to 1, especially when there are many parameters relative to the size of the dataset

For these reasons, the Laplace approximation is usually not used for HMMs.

Stolke and Omohundro's method

In the famous paper *HMM induction by Bayesian model merging* Stolke and Omohundro present a new technique for approximating the Bayesian integrals of HMMs. Consider the case of having all the states of the HMM to be observed and the priors to be Dirichlet distributions. In this case, when learning the parameters using Bayesian learning, the posteriors are also going to be Dirichlet distributions, and then the evidence integral can be represented as a product of Dirichlet integrals, which can be easily computed. Therefore, in a sense, we can say that the reason for the intractability of evidence integrals is the fact that the states and parameters are hidden.

Stolke and Omohundro's method proposed to find the single most likely sequence of hidden states using a Viterbi-like algorithm and using this sequence as observed states. Using these observed values, we can easily do evidence integrals. The method proposes to iterate between these two steps, incrementally searching over model structures, merging or splitting states based on comparisons of this approximate evidence. In their paper, Stolke and Omohundro show that this method of trading off integration over hidden variables by integrating over parameters is able to get good results.

Variational methods

Variational methods are another very common method used for approximating distributions. The general idea is to start by choosing a simpler family of distributions and then try to find the hyperparameters of this distribution such that the distribution is as close as possible to our original distribution. There are different metrics that are used to determine the closeness of two distributions; the most commonly used metric is Kullback-Leiber divergence. This method basically converts an inference problem into an optimization problem where we try to minimize our divergence metric.

In the case of HMMs, we usually make an assumption that the hidden states are independent of the parameters of the model. This allows us to approximate distributions over both the hidden states and parameters simultaneously. More specifically, the evidence can be lower bounded by applying Jenson's inequality twice:

$$
\begin{aligned}
\log P(\mathcal{D}|\mathcal{M}) = \log &\int d\theta P(\mathcal{D}, \theta | \mathcal{M}) \\
\geq &\int d\theta Q(\theta) \log \frac{P(\mathcal{D}, \theta | \mathcal{M})}{Q(\theta)} \\
= &\int d\theta Q(\theta) \left[\log P(\mathcal{D}|\theta, \mathcal{M}) + \log \frac{P(\theta | \mathcal{M})}{Q(\theta)} \right] \\
\geq &\int d\theta Q(\theta) \left[\sum_{\mathcal{S}} Q(\mathcal{S}) \log \frac{P(\mathcal{S}, \mathcal{D}|\theta, \mathcal{M})}{Q(\mathcal{S})} + \log \frac{P(\theta | \mathcal{M})}{Q(\theta)} \right] \\
\equiv &\ \mathcal{F}(Q(\theta), Q(\mathcal{S}))
\end{aligned}
$$

The variational Bayesian approach iteratively maximizes $\mathcal{F}$ as a functional of the two free distributions, $Q(S)$ and $Q(\theta)$. In the preceding equations, we can see that this maximization is equivalent to minimizing the KL divergence between $Q(S)Q(\theta)$ and the joint posterior over hidden states and the $P(S,\theta \mid D,M)$ parameters. David MacKay first presented a variational Bayesian approach to learning in HMMs. He assumed the prior to be a Dirichlet distribution, making the assumption that the parameters are independent of the hidden states, he showed that the optimal $Q(\theta)$ is a Dirichlet distribution. Furthermore, he showed that the optimal $Q(S)$ could be obtained by applying the forward-backward algorithm to an HMM with pseudo-parameters given by $\theta^{*} = \exp\{\int d\theta Q(\theta) \log \theta\}$, which can be evaluated for Dirichlet distributions. Thus the whole variational Bayesian method can be implemented as a simple modification of the Baum-Welch algorithm. Essentially we can state that the variational Bayesian method is a combination of special cases of both the MAP approach and Stolke and Omohundro's approach. This is very promising, especially given that it has been used successfully for non-trivial model-structure learning in other models; its potential has not been fully explored for HMMs and their extensions.

Code

Currently, there are no packages in Python that support learning using Bayesian learning and it would be really difficult to write the complete code to fit in this book. And even though there are a lot of advantages to using Bayesian learning, it is usually computationally infeasible in a lot of cases. For these reasons, we are skipping the code for Bayesian learning in HMMs.

Summary

In this chapter, we talked about applying Bayesian learning in the case of learning parameters in HMMs. Bayesian learning has a few benefits over the maximum-likelihood estimator, but it turns out to be computationally quite expensive except when we have closed-form solutions. Closed-form solutions are only possible when we use conjugate priors. In the following chapters, we will discuss detailed applications of HMMs for a wide variety of problems.

6
Time Series Predicting

In the previous chapters, we discussed **Hidden Markov Models** (**HMMs**) and various algorithms associated with inference in great theoretical detail. From this chapter onward, we will be discussing the use of HMMs.

HMMs are capable of predicting and analyzing time-based phenomena. Because of this, they can be used in fields such as speech recognition, natural language processing, and financial market prediction. In this chapter, we will be looking into applications of HMMs in the field of financial market analysis, mainly stock price prediction.

Stock price prediction using HMM

Stock market prediction has been one of the more active research areas in the past, given the obvious interest of a lot of major companies. Historically, various machine learning algorithms have been applied with varying degrees of success. However, stock forecasting is still severely limited due to its non-stationary, seasonal, and unpredictable nature. Predicting forecasts from just the previous stock data is an even more challenging task since it ignores several outlying factors.

As seen previously, HMMs are capable of modeling hidden state transitions from the sequential observed data. The problem of stock prediction can also be thought as following the same pattern. The price of the stock depends upon a multitude of factors which generally remain invisible to the investor (hidden variables). The transition between the underlaying factors change based on company policy and decisions, its financial conditions, and management decisions, and these affect the price of the stock (observed data). So HMMs are a natural fit to the problem of price prediction.

In this chapter, we will try to predict the stock prices for Alphabet Inc. (GOOGL), **Facebook** (**FB**), and **Apple Inc.** (**AAPL**).

Collecting stock price data

We will use pystock data (`http://data.pystock.com`) to get the historical stock prices data. Every day, before the US stock exchanges open at 9:30 EST/EDT, the pystock crawler collects the stock prices and financial reports, and pushes the data, such as the previous day's opening price, closing price, highest price, and lowest price for a given stock, to the repository. This data is day-based, meaning we won't be having any hour or minute-level data.

Let's try to download the `pystock` data for a given year. As the dataset is large, we will create a Python script to download the data for a given year and we can run the program simultaneously for three different years to download all the data in parallel:

```python
"""
Usage: get_data.py --year=<year>
"""
import requests
import os
from docopt import docopt

# docopt helps parsing the command line argument in
# a simple manner (http://docopt.org/)
args = docopt(doc=__doc__, argv=None,
            help=True, version=None,
            options_first=False)

year = args['--year']

# Create directory if not present
year_directory_name = 'data/{year}'.format(year=year)
if not os.path.exists(year_directory_name):
    os.makedirs(year_directory_name)

# Fetching file list for the corresponding year
year_data_files = requests.get(
    'http://data.pystock.com/{year}/index.txt'.format(year=year)
).text.strip().split('\n')

for data_file_name in year_data_files:
    file_location = '{year_directory_name}/{data_file_name}'.format(
        year_directory_name=year_directory_name,
        data_file_name=data_file_name)

    with open(file_location, 'wb+') as data_file:
        print('>>> Downloading \t
{file_location}'.format(file_location=file_location))
        data_file_content = requests.get(
```

```
'http://data.pystock.com/{year}/{data_file_name}'.format(year=year,
data_file_name=data_file_name)
        ).content
        print('<<< Download Completed \t
{file_location}'.format(file_location=file_location))
        data_file.write(data_file_content)
```

Run the following scripts simultaneously for three different years:

```
python get_data.py --year 2015
python get_data.py --year 2016
python get_data.py --year 2017
```

Once the data is downloaded, let's try to get all the data for each of the preceding stated stocks by combining data corresponding to all the years:

```
"""
Usage: parse_data.py --company=<company>
"""
import os
import tarfile
import pandas as pd
from pandas import errors as pd_errors
from functools import reduce
from docopt import docopt

args = docopt(doc=__doc__, argv=None,
              help=True, version=None,
              options_first=False)

years = [2015, 2016, 2017]
company = args['--company']


# Getting the data files list
data_files_list = []
for year in years:
    year_directory = 'data/{year}'.format(year=year)
    for file in os.listdir(year_directory):
data_files_list.append('{year_directory}/{file}'.format(year_directory=year
_directory, file=file))


def parse_data(file_name, company_symbol):
    """
    Returns data for the corresponding company

    :param file_name: name of the tar file
```

```
    :param company_symbol: company symbol
    :type file_name: str
    :type company_symbol: str
    :return: dataframe for the corresponding company data
    :rtype: pd.DataFrame
    """
    tar = tarfile.open(file_name)
    try:
        price_report = pd.read_csv(tar.extractfile('prices.csv'))
        company_price_data = price_report[price_report['symbol'] ==
company_symbol]
        return company_price_data
    except (KeyError, pd_errors.EmptyDataError):
        return pd.DataFrame()


# Getting the complete data for a given company
company_data = reduce(lambda df, file_name: df.append(parse_data(file_name,
company)),
                      data_files_list,
                      pd.DataFrame())
company_data = company_data.sort_values(by=['date'])

# Create folder for company data if does not exists
if not os.path.exists('data/company_data'):
    os.makedirs('data/company_data')

# Write data to a CSV file
company_data.to_csv('data/company_data/{company}.csv'.format(company=compan
y),
                    columns=['date', 'open', 'high', 'low', 'close',
'volume', 'adj_close'],
                    index=False)
```

Run the following scripts to create a `.csv` file containing all the historical data for the GOOGL, FB, and AAPL stocks:

```
python parse_data.py --company GOOGL
python parse_data.py --company FB
python parse_data.py --company AAPL
```

Features for stock price prediction

Once we have the data for each of the stock prices, we want to predict the price of the stock. As we mentioned earlier, we have very limited features for each day, namely the opening price of stock for that day, closing price, highest price of stock, and lowest price of stock. So we are going to use them to compute the stock prices. Generally, we want to compute the closing stock price for a day, given the opening stock price for that day, and previous some *d* days data. Our predictor would have a latency of *d* days.

Let's create a predictor called `StockPredictor`, which will contain all the logic to predict the stock price for a given company during a given day.

Instead of directly using the opening, closing, low, and high prices of a stock, let's try to extract the fractional changes in each of them that would be used to train our HMM. As we move further, the reason for choosing these features will become clearer. We could define three parameters as follows:

$$frac_{change} = \frac{(close - open)}{open}$$

$$frac_{high} = \frac{(high - open)}{open}$$

$$frac_{low} = \frac{(open - low)}{open}$$

So, for the stock price predictor HMM, we can represent a single observation as a vector these parameters, namely $X_t = <frac_{change}, frac_{high}, frac_{low}>$:

```python
import pandas as pd

class StockPredictor(object):
    def __init__(self, company, n_latency_days=10):
        self._init_logger()

        self.company = company
        self.n_latency_days = n_latency_days
        self.data = pd.read_csv(
            'data/company_data/{company}.csv'.format(company=self.company))


    def _init_logger(self):
        self._logger = logging.getLogger(__name__)
```

```
handler = logging.StreamHandler()
formatter = logging.Formatter(
    '%(asctime)s %(name)-12s %(levelname)-8s %(message)s')
handler.setFormatter(formatter)
self._logger.addHandler(handler)
self._logger.setLevel(logging.DEBUG)


@staticmethod
def _extract_features(data):
    open_price = np.array(data['open'])
    close_price = np.array(data['close'])
    high_price = np.array(data['high'])
    low_price = np.array(data['low'])

    # Compute the fraction change in close, high and low prices
    # which would be used a feature
    frac_change = (close_price - open_price) / open_price
    frac_high = (high_price - open_price) / open_price
    frac_low = (open_price - low_price) / open_price

    return np.column_stack((frac_change, frac_high, frac_low))


# Predictor for GOOGL stocks
stock_predictor = StockPredictor(company='GOOGL')
```

Predicting price using HMM

Once we extract the features from the data, we can now move on to predicting the price of the stock. We want to predict the closing price of a stock on a particular day, given the opening price of the stock on that day and stock prices of previous days.

The first step would be to train an HMM to compute the parameters from the given sequence of observations that we computed earlier. As the observations are a vector of continuous random variables, we have to assume that the emission probability distribution is continuous. For simplicity, let's assume that it is a multinomial Gaussian distribution with parameters (μ and Σ). So we have to determine the following parameters for the transition matrix, A, prior probabilities, π, along with μ and Σ which represent the multinomial Gaussian distribution.

For now, let's assume that we have four hidden states. In the coming sections, we will look into ways of finding the optimal number of hidden states. We will use the GaussianHMM class provided by the hmmlearn package as our HMM, and we will try to perform parameter estimation using the fit() method provided by it:

```python
from hmmlearn.hmm import GaussianHMM


class StockPredictor(object):
    def __init__(self, company, n_latency_days=10, n_hidden_states=4):
        self._init_logger()

        self.company = company
        self.n_latency_days = n_latency_days

        self.hmm = GaussianHMM(n_components=n_hidden_states)

        self.data = pd.read_csv(
            'data/company_data/{company}.csv'.format(company=self.company))

    def fit(self):
        self._logger.info('>>> Extracting Features')
        feature_vector = StockPredictor._extract_features(self.data)
        self._logger.info('Features extraction Completed <<<')

        self.hmm.fit(feature_vector)
```

In machine learning, we divide the entire dataset into two categories. The first set, the training dataset, is used to train the model. The second set, the test dataset, is used to provide an unbiased evaluation of a final model fit on the training dataset. Separating the training dataset from the test dataset prevents us from overfitting the data to the model. So, in our case, we would also split the dataset into two categories, train_data for training the model and test_data for evaluating the model. To do so, we will use the train_test_split method provided by the sklearn.model_selection module:

 train_test_split can split arrays or matrices into random train and test subsets. As we are training our HMM with sequential data, we do not want to randomly split the data. To prevent random splitting of the test and train data, pass shuffle=False as the argument.

```python
from sklearn.model_selection import train_test_split


class StockPredictor(object):
    def __init__(self, company, test_size=0.33,
                 n_latency_days=10, n_hidden_states=4):
```

```
        self._init_logger()

        self.company = company
        self.n_latency_days = n_latency_days

        self.hmm = GaussianHMM(n_components=n_hidden_states)

        self._split_train_test_data(test_size)

    def _split_train_test_data(self, test_size):
        data = pd.read_csv(
            'data/company_data/{company}.csv'.format(company=self.company))
        _train_data, test_data = train_test_split(
            data, test_size=test_size, shuffle=False)

        self._train_data = _train_data
        self._test_data = test_data

    def fit(self):
        self._logger.info('>>> Extracting Features')
        feature_vector = StockPredictor._extract_features(self._train_data)
        self._logger.info('Features extraction Completed <<<')

        self.hmm.fit(feature_vector)
```

Once your model is trained, we need to predict the stock closing price. As we mentioned earlier, we want to predict the stock closing price for a day given that we know the opening price. This means that if we are able to predict $frac_{change}$ for a given day, we can compute the closing price as follows:

$$closing = open * (1 + frac_{change})$$

Thus our problem boils down to computing the $X_{t+1} = <frac_{change}, frac_{high}, frac_{low}>$ observation vector for a day given the observation data for t days, $x_1,...,x_t$, and the parameters of the HMM $\theta = \{\mathbf{A}, \pi, \phi\}$, which is finding the value of X_{t+1} that maximizes the posterior probability $P(X_{t+1}|X_1,...,X_t,\theta)$:

$$
\begin{aligned}
X_{t+1} &= argmax_{X_{t+1}} P(X_{t+1}|X_1,\ldots,X_t,\theta) \\
&= argmax_{X_{t+1}} \frac{P(X1,\ldots,X_t,X_{t+1},\theta)}{P(X1,\ldots,X_t,\theta)} \\
&= argmax_{X_{t+1}} P(X1,\ldots,X_t,X_{t+1}|\theta)P(\theta) \\
&= argmax_{X_{t+1}} P(X1,\ldots,X_t,X_{t+1}|\theta)
\end{aligned}
$$

As you can see, once you remove all the parameters that are independent of X_{t+1} from the maximization equation, we are left with the problem of finding the value of X_{t+1}, which optimizes the probability of $P(X_1,...,X_{t+1}|\theta)$. We came across this problem in Chapter 4, *Parameter Learning using Maximum Likelihood*, while evaluating the probability of a sequence given the model parameters. It can be computed efficiently using the forward-backward algorithm.

If we assume $frac_{change}$ is a continuous variable, the optimization of the problem would be computationally difficult. So we can divide these fractional changes into some discrete values ranging between two finite variables (as stated in the following table) and try to find a set of fractional changes, $< frac_{change}, frac_{high}, frac_{low} >$, that would maximize the probability, $P(X_1,...,X_{t+1}|\theta)$:

Observation	Minimum value	Maximum value	Number of points
$frac_{change}$	-0.1	0.1	20
$frac_{high}$	0	0.1	10
$frac_{low}$	0	0.1	10

So, with the preceding discrete set of values, we need to run (20 x 10 x 10 =) 2,000 operations:

```
def _compute_all_possible_outcomes(self, n_steps_frac_change,
                                   n_steps_frac_high,
    n_steps_frac_low):
        frac_change_range = np.linspace(-0.1, 0.1, n_steps_frac_change)
        frac_high_range = np.linspace(0, 0.1, n_steps_frac_high)
        frac_low_range = np.linspace(0, 0.1, n_steps_frac_low)

        self._possible_outcomes = np.array(list(itertools.product(
            frac_change_range, frac_high_range, frac_low_range)))
```

Now we can implement the method to predict the closing price, as follows:

```
def _get_most_probable_outcome(self, day_index):
        previous_data_start_index = max(0, day_index - self.n_latency_days)
        previous_data_end_index = max(0, day_index - 1)
        previous_data = self._test_data.iloc[previous_data_end_index:
    previous_data_start_index]
        previous_data_features = StockPredictor._extract_features(
            previous_data)

        outcome_score = []
        for possible_outcome in self._possible_outcomes:
            total_data = np.row_stack(
                (previous_data_features, possible_outcome))
```

```
                    outcome_score.append(self.hmm.score(total_data))
            most_probable_outcome = self._possible_outcomes[np.argmax(
                outcome_score)]

            return most_probable_outcome

    def predict_close_price(self, day_index):
        open_price = self._test_data.iloc[day_index]['open']
        predicted_frac_change, _, _ = self._get_most_probable_outcome(
            day_index)
        return open_price * (1 + predicted_frac_change)
```

Let's try to predict the closing price for a some days and plot both the curves:

```
"""
Usage: analyse_data.py --company=<company>
"""
import warnings
import logging
import itertools
import pandas as pd
import numpy as np
import matplotlib.pyplot as plt
from hmmlearn.hmm import GaussianHMM
from sklearn.model_selection import train_test_split
from tqdm import tqdm
from docopt import docopt

args = docopt(doc=__doc__, argv=None, help=True,
              version=None, options_first=False)

# Supress warning in hmmlearn
warnings.filterwarnings("ignore")
# Change plot style to ggplot (for better and more aesthetic visualisation)
plt.style.use('ggplot')


class StockPredictor(object):
    def __init__(self, company, test_size=0.33,
                 n_hidden_states=4, n_latency_days=10,
                 n_steps_frac_change=50, n_steps_frac_high=10,
                 n_steps_frac_low=10):
        self._init_logger()

        self.company = company
        self.n_latency_days = n_latency_days

        self.hmm = GaussianHMM(n_components=n_hidden_states)
```

```
        self._split_train_test_data(test_size)

        self._compute_all_possible_outcomes(
            n_steps_frac_change, n_steps_frac_high, n_steps_frac_low)

    def _init_logger(self):
        self._logger = logging.getLogger(__name__)
        handler = logging.StreamHandler()
        formatter = logging.Formatter(
            '%(asctime)s %(name)-12s %(levelname)-8s %(message)s')
        handler.setFormatter(formatter)
        self._logger.addHandler(handler)
        self._logger.setLevel(logging.DEBUG)

    def _split_train_test_data(self, test_size):
        data = pd.read_csv(
            'data/company_data/{company}.csv'.format(company=self.company))
        _train_data, test_data = train_test_split(
            data, test_size=test_size, shuffle=False)

        self._train_data = _train_data
        self._test_data = test_data

    @staticmethod
    def _extract_features(data):
        open_price = np.array(data['open'])
        close_price = np.array(data['close'])
        high_price = np.array(data['high'])
        low_price = np.array(data['low'])

        # Compute the fraction change in close, high and low prices
        # which would be used a feature
        frac_change = (close_price - open_price) / open_price
        frac_high = (high_price - open_price) / open_price
        frac_low = (open_price - low_price) / open_price

        return np.column_stack((frac_change, frac_high, frac_low))

    def fit(self):
        self._logger.info('>>> Extracting Features')
        feature_vector = StockPredictor._extract_features(self._train_data)
        self._logger.info('Features extraction Completed <<<')

        self.hmm.fit(feature_vector)

    def _compute_all_possible_outcomes(self, n_steps_frac_change,
                                       n_steps_frac_high,
n_steps_frac_low):
```

```
                frac_change_range = np.linspace(-0.1, 0.1, n_steps_frac_change)
                frac_high_range = np.linspace(0, 0.1, n_steps_frac_high)
                frac_low_range = np.linspace(0, 0.1, n_steps_frac_low)

                self._possible_outcomes = np.array(list(itertools.product(
                    frac_change_range, frac_high_range, frac_low_range)))

        def _get_most_probable_outcome(self, day_index):
                previous_data_start_index = max(0, day_index - self.n_latency_days)
                previous_data_end_index = max(0, day_index - 1)
                previous_data = self._test_data.iloc[previous_data_end_index:
        previous_data_start_index]
                previous_data_features = StockPredictor._extract_features(
                    previous_data)

                outcome_score = []
                for possible_outcome in self._possible_outcomes:
                    total_data = np.row_stack(
                        (previous_data_features, possible_outcome))
                    outcome_score.append(self.hmm.score(total_data))
                most_probable_outcome = self._possible_outcomes[np.argmax(
                    outcome_score)]

                return most_probable_outcome

        def predict_close_price(self, day_index):
                open_price = self._test_data.iloc[day_index]['open']
                predicted_frac_change, _, _ = self._get_most_probable_outcome(
                    day_index)
                return open_price * (1 + predicted_frac_change)

        def predict_close_prices_for_days(self, days, with_plot=False):
                predicted_close_prices = []
                for day_index in tqdm(range(days)):
        predicted_close_prices.append(self.predict_close_price(day_index))

                if with_plot:
                    test_data = self._test_data[0: days]
                    days = np.array(test_data['date'], dtype="datetime64[ms]")
                    actual_close_prices = test_data['close']

                    fig = plt.figure()

                    axes = fig.add_subplot(111)
                    axes.plot(days, actual_close_prices, 'bo-', label="actual")
                    axes.plot(days, predicted_close_prices, 'r+-',
        label="predicted")
                    axes.set_title('{company}'.format(company=self.company))
```

```
        fig.autofmt_xdate()

        plt.legend()
        plt.show()

    return predicted_close_prices


stock_predictor = StockPredictor(company=args['--company'])
stock_predictor.fit()
stock_predictor.predict_close_prices_for_days(500, with_plot=True)
```

The output is as follows:

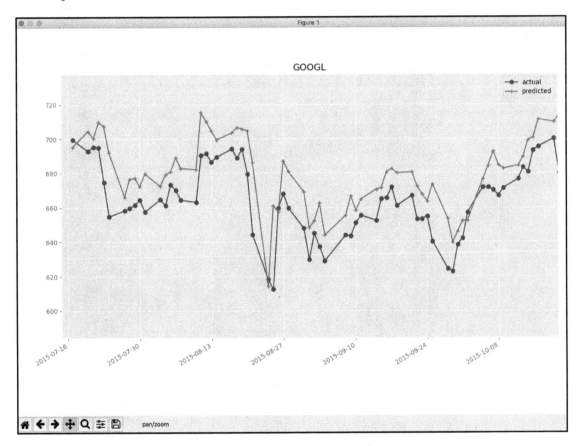

Summary

In this chapter, we predicted the price of stocks using HMM. We applied the parameter-estimation and evaluation-of-model methods to determine the closing price of a stocks. Using HMM in stock market analysis is just another example of the application of HMM in analyzing time series data.

In the next chapter, we will look at an interesting application of HMM in the field of natural language processing.

7
Natural Language Processing

Automatic speech recognition has a lot of potential applications, such as audio transcription, dictation, audio search, and virtual assistants. I am sure that everyone has interacted with at least one of the virtual assistants by now, be it Apple's Siri, Amazon's Alexa, or Google's Assistant. At the core of all these speech recognition systems are a set of statistical models over the different words or sounds in a language. And since speech has a temporal structure, HMMs are the most natural framework to model it.

HMMs are virtually at the core of all speech recognition systems and the core concepts in modeling haven't changed much in a long time. But over time, a lot of sophisticated techniques have been developed to build better systems. In the following sections, we will try to cover the main concepts leading to the development of these systems.

Part-of-speech tagging

The first problem that we will look into is known as **part-of-speech tagging** (**POS tagging**). According to Wikipedia, POS tagging, also known as **grammatical tagging** or **word-category disambiguation**, is the process of marking up a word in a text as corresponding to a particular part of speech based on both its definition and its context, that is, its relationship with adjacent and related words in a phrase, sentence, or paragraph. A simpler version of this, which is usually taught in schools, is classifying words as noun, verbs, adjectives, and so on.

POS tagging is not as easy as it sounds because the same word can take different parts of speech in different contexts. A simple example of this is the word *dogs*. The word *dogs* is usually considered a noun, but in the following sentence, it acts like a verb:

The sailor dogs the hatch.

Correct grammatical tagging will reflect that *dogs* is used as a verb here, not as the more common plural noun. Grammatical context is one way to determine this; semantic analysis can also be used to infer that *sailor* and *hatch* implicate *dogs* as:

- In the nautical context
- An action applied to the object *hatch*

In teaching English, generally only nine parts of speech are taught: noun, verb, article, adjective, preposition, pronoun, adverb, conjunction, and interjection. But we can divide words into more categories and subcategories for finer-grained tagging. For example, nouns can be sub-categorized into plural, possessive, and singular. Similarly, verbs can be sub-categorized on the basis of tense, aspect, and so on. In general, computer-based POS tagging systems are able to distinguish 50 to 150 separate parts of speech for English. Work on stochastic methods for tagging Koine Greek has used over 1,000 parts of speech and found that about as many words were ambiguous there as in English.

Code

For the code example, we will use the `pomegranate` library to build an HMM for POS tagging. Pomegranate can be installed by running the following on the command line:

```
pip install pomegranate
```

In this example, we will not go into the details of the statistical POS tagger. The data we are using is a copy of the Brown corpus. The Brown corpus contains 500 samples of English-language text, totaling roughly 1,000,000 words, compiled from works published in the United States in 1961.

Getting data

Let's start by defining some functions to read the data from the `corpus` files:

```python
# Imports
import random
from itertools import chain
from collections import Counter, defaultdict

import numpy as np
import matplotlib.pyplot as plt
from pomegranate import State, HiddenMarkovModel, DiscreteDistribution


Sentence = namedtuple("Sentence", "words tags")


def read_data(filename):
    """
    Function to read tagged sentence data.

    Parameters
    ----------
    filename: str
        The path to the file from where to read the data.

    """
    with open(filename, 'r') as f:
        sentence_lines = [l.split("\n") for l in f.read().split("\n\n")]
    return OrderedDict(((s[0], Sentence(*zip(*[l.strip().split("\t") for l
in s[1:]])))
                        for s in sentence_lines if s[0]))

def read_tags(filename):
    """
    Function to read a list of word tag classes.

    Parameters
    ----------
    filename: str
        The path to the file from where to read the tags.
    """
    with open(filename, 'r') as f:
        tags = f.read().split("\n")
    return frozenset(tags)
```

Let's now define a couple of classes, `Subset` and `Dataset`, to make it easier to handle the data:

```
class Subset(namedtuple("BaseSet", "sentences keys vocab X tagset Y N
stream")):
    """
    Class to handle a subset of the whole data. This is required when we
split the
    data into training and test sets.
    """
    def __new__(cls, sentences, keys):
        word_sequences = tuple([sentences[k].words for k in keys])
        tag_sequences = tuple([sentences[k].tags for k in keys])
        wordset = frozenset(chain(*word_sequences))
        tagset = frozenset(chain(*tag_sequences))
        N = sum(1 for _ in chain(*(sentences[k].words for k in keys)))
        stream = tuple(zip(chain(*word_sequences), chain(*tag_sequences)))
        return super().__new__(cls, {k: sentences[k] for k in keys}, keys,
wordset,
                                word_sequences, tagset, tag_sequences, N,
stream.__iter__)

    def __len__(self):
        return len(self.sentences)

    def __iter__(self):
        return iter(self.sentences.items())

class Dataset(namedtuple("_Dataset", "sentences keys vocab X tagset Y" +
                                "training_set testing_set N stream")):
    """
    Class to represent the data in structured form for easy processing.
    """
    def __new__(cls, tagfile, datafile, train_test_split=0.8, seed=112890):
        tagset = read_tags(tagfile)
        sentences = read_data(datafile)
        keys = tuple(sentences.keys())
        wordset = frozenset(chain(*[s.words for s in sentences.values()]))
        word_sequences = tuple([sentences[k].words for k in keys])
        tag_sequences = tuple([sentences[k].tags for k in keys])
        N = sum(1 for _ in chain(*(s.words for s in sentences.values())))

        # split data into train/test sets
        _keys = list(keys)
        if seed is not None:
            random.seed(seed)
        random.shuffle(_keys)
        split = int(train_test_split * len(_keys))
```

```
        training_data = Subset(sentences, _keys[:split])
        testing_data = Subset(sentences, _keys[split:])
        stream = tuple(zip(chain(*word_sequences), chain(*tag_sequences)))
        return super().__new__(cls, dict(sentences), keys, wordset,
word_sequences, tagset,
                                tag_sequences, training_data, testing_data,
N, stream.__iter__)

    def __len__(self):
        return len(self.sentences)

    def __iter__(self):
        return iter(self.sentences.items())
```

Now, let's try to initialize the `Dataset` class and see how it works:

```
>>> data = Dataset("tags-universal.txt", "brown-universal.txt",
train_test_split=0.8)

>>> print("There are {} sentences in the corpus.".format(len(data)))
There are 57340 sentences in the corpus.
>>> print("There are {} sentences in the training
set.".format(len(data.training_set)))
There are 45872 sentences in the training set.
>>> print("There are {} sentences in the testing
set.".format(len(data.testing_set)))
There are 11468 sentences in the testing set.
```

Exploring the data

Let's now explore the data to better understand how our classes store the information. We have randomly selected the `b100-38532` key:

```
>>> key = 'b100-38532'
>>> print("Sentence: {}".format(key))
Sentence: b100-38532
>>> print("words: {!s}".format(data.sentences[key].words))\
words: ('Perhaps', 'it', 'was', 'right', ';', ';')
>>> print("tags: {!s}".format(data.sentences[key].tags))
tags: ('ADV', 'PRON', 'VERB', 'ADJ', '.', '.')
```

We can also check the unique elements in the `corpus`:

```
>>> print("There are a total of {} samples of {} unique words in the
corpus.".format(
            data.N, len(data.vocab)))
There are a total of 1161192 samples of 56057 unique words in the corpus.
```

```
>>> print("There are {} samples of {} unique words in the training
set.".format(
            data.training_set.N, len(data.training_set.vocab)))
There are 928458 samples of 50536 unique words in the training set.

>>> print("There are {} samples of {} unique words in the testing
set.".format(
            data.testing_set.N, len(data.testing_set.vocab)))
There are 232734 samples of 25112 unique words in the testing set.
>>> print("There are {} words in the test set that are missing in the
training set.".format(
            len(data.testing_set.vocab - data.training_set.vocab)))
There are 5521 words in the test set that are missing in the training set.
```

We can also use the X and Y attributes of the `Dataset` class to access the words and the corresponding tags:

```
>>> for i in range(2):
...        print("Sentence {}:".format(i + 1), data.X[i])
...        print("Labels {}:".format(i + 1), data.Y[i], "\n")
Sentence 1: ('Mr.', 'Podger', 'had', 'thanked', 'him', 'gravely', ',',
'and', 'now', 'he', 'made', 'use', 'of', 'the', 'advice', '.')
Labels 1: ('NOUN', 'NOUN', 'VERB', 'VERB', 'PRON', 'ADV', '.', 'CONJ',
'ADV', 'PRON', 'VERB', 'NOUN', 'ADP', 'DET', 'NOUN', '.')

Sentence 2: ('But', 'there', 'seemed', 'to', 'be', 'some', 'difference',
'of', 'opinion', 'as', 'to', 'how', 'far', 'the', 'board', 'should', 'go',
',', 'and', 'whose', 'advice', 'it', 'should', 'follow', '.')
Labels 2: ('CONJ', 'PRT', 'VERB', 'PRT', 'VERB', 'DET', 'NOUN', 'ADP',
'NOUN', 'ADP', 'ADP', 'ADV', 'ADV', 'DET', 'NOUN', 'VERB','VERB', '.',
'CONJ', 'DET', 'NOUN', 'PRON', 'VERB', 'VERB', '.')
```

We can also use the `stream` method to iterate over pairs of a word and its tag:

```
>>> for i, pair in enumerate(data.stream()):
...        print(pair)
...        if i > 3:
...            break
('Podger', 'NOUN')
('had', 'VERB')
('thanked', 'VERB')
('him', 'PRON')
```

Finding the most frequent tag

Now, just to compare the performance of our HMM model, let's build a **most frequent class tagger** (**MFC Tagger**). We start by defining a function to count the pairs of tags and words:

```
def pair_counts(tags, words):
    d = defaultdict(lambda: defaultdict(int))
    for tag, word in zip(tags, words):
        d[tag][word] += 1
    return d
tags = [tag for i, (word, tag) in enumerate(data.training_set.stream())]
words = [word for i, (word, tag) in enumerate(data.training_set.stream())]
```

Now, let's define the MFCTagger class:

```
FakeState = namedtuple('FakeState', 'name')

class MFCTagger:
    missing = FakeState(name = '<MISSING>')
    def __init__(self, table):
        self.table = defaultdict(lambda: MFCTagger.missing)
        self.table.update({word: FakeState(name=tag) for word, tag in
table.items()})
    def viterbi(self, seq):
        """This method simplifies predictions by matching the Pomegranate
viterbi() interface"""
        return 0., list(enumerate(["<start>"] + [self.table[w] for w in
seq] + ["<end>"]))
tags = [tag for i, (word, tag) in enumerate(data.training_set.stream())]
words = [word for i, (word, tag) in enumerate(data.training_set.stream())]

word_counts = pair_counts(words, tags)
mfc_table = dict((word, max(tags.keys(), key=lambda key: tags[key])) for
word, tags in word_counts.items())

mfc_model = MFCTagger(mfc_table)
```

Here are some helper functions to make predictions from the model:

```
def replace_unknown(sequence):
    return [w if w in data.training_set.vocab else 'nan' for w in sequence]

def simplify_decoding(X, model):
    _, state_path = model.viterbi(replace_unknown(X))
    return [state[1].name for state in state_path[1:-1]]

>>> for key in data.testing_set.keys[:2]:
```

```
...         print("Sentence Key: {}\n".format(key))
...         print("Predicted labels:\n------------------")
...         print(simplify_decoding(data.sentences[key].words, mfc_model))
...         print()
...         print("Actual labels:\n--------------")
...         print(data.sentences[key].tags)
...         print("\n")
```

```
Sentence Key: b100-28144

Predicted labels:
-----------------
['CONJ', 'NOUN', 'NUM', '.', 'NOUN', 'NUM', '.', 'NOUN', 'NUM', '.', 'CONJ', 'NOUN', 'NUM', '.', '.', 'NOUN', '.', '.']

Actual labels:
--------------
('CONJ', 'NOUN', 'NUM', '.', 'NOUN', 'NUM', '.', 'NOUN', 'NUM', '.', 'CONJ', 'NOUN', 'NUM', '.', '.', 'NOUN', '.', '.')


Sentence Key: b100-23146

Predicted labels:
-----------------
['PRON', 'VERB', 'DET', 'NOUN', 'ADP', 'ADJ', 'ADJ', 'NOUN', 'VERB', 'VERB', '.', 'ADP', 'VERB', 'DET', 'NOUN', 'ADP', 'NOUN',
'ADP', 'DET', 'NOUN', '.']

Actual labels:
--------------
('PRON', 'VERB', 'DET', 'NOUN', 'ADP', 'ADJ', 'ADJ', 'NOUN', 'VERB', 'VERB', '.', 'ADP', 'VERB', 'DET', 'NOUN', 'ADP', 'NOUN',
'ADP', 'DET', 'NOUN', '.')
```

Evaluating model accuracy

To check how well our model performs, let's evaluate the accuracy of our model:

```
def accuracy(X, Y, model):
    correct = total_predictions = 0
    for observations, actual_tags in zip(X, Y):
        # The model.viterbi call in simplify_decoding will return None if
the HMM
        # raises an error (for example, if a test sentence contains a word
that
        # is out of vocabulary for the training set). Any exception counts
the
        # full sentence as an error (which makes this a conservative
estimate).
        try:
            most_likely_tags = simplify_decoding(observations, model)
            correct += sum(p == t for p, t in zip(most_likely_tags,
actual_tags))
        except:
            pass
        total_predictions += len(observations)
```

```
        return correct / total_predictions

>>> mfc_training_acc = accuracy(data.training_set.X, data.training_set.Y,
mfc_model)
>>> print("Training accuracy mfc_model: {:.2f}%".format(100 *
mfc_training_acc))
Training accuracy mfc_model: 95.72%

>>> mfc_testing_acc = accuracy(data.testing_set.X, data.testing_set.Y,
mfc_model)
>>> print("Testing accuracy mfc_model: {:.2f}%".format(100 *
mfc_testing_acc))
Testing accuracy mfc_model: 93.01%
```

An HMM-based tagger

Now, we will try to build a POS tagger using HMM and hopefully it will improve our prediction performance. We will first define some helper functions:

```
def unigram_counts(sequences):
    return Counter(sequences)

tags = [tag for i, (word, tag) in enumerate(data.training_set.stream())]
tag_unigrams = unigram_counts(tags)

def bigram_counts(sequences):
    d = Counter(sequences)
    return d

tags = [tag for i, (word, tag) in enumerate(data.stream())]
o = [(tags[i],tags[i+1]) for i in range(0,len(tags)-2,2)]
tag_bigrams = bigram_counts(o)

def starting_counts(sequences):
    d = Counter(sequences)
    return d

tags = [tag for i, (word, tag) in enumerate(data.stream())]
starts_tag = [i[0] for i in data.Y]
tag_starts = starting_counts(starts_tag)

def ending_counts(sequences):
    d = Counter(sequences)
    return d

end_tag = [i[len(i)-1] for i in data.Y]
tag_ends = ending_counts(end_tag)
```

Let's build the model now:

```
basic_model = HiddenMarkovModel(name="base-hmm-tagger")

tags = [tag for i, (word, tag) in enumerate(data.stream())]
words = [word for i, (word, tag) in enumerate(data.stream())]

tags_count=unigram_counts(tags)
tag_words_count=pair_counts(tags,words)

starting_tag_list=[i[0] for i in data.Y]
ending_tag_list=[i[-1] for i in data.Y]

starting_tag_count=starting_counts(starting_tag_list)#the number of times a
tag occurred at the start
ending_tag_count=ending_counts(ending_tag_list)        #the number of times a
tag occurred at the end

to_pass_states = []
for tag, words_dict in tag_words_count.items():
    total = float(sum(words_dict.values()))
    distribution = {word: count/total for word, count in
words_dict.items()}
    tag_emissions = DiscreteDistribution(distribution)
    tag_state = State(tag_emissions, name=tag)
    to_pass_states.append(tag_state)

basic_model.add_states()

start_prob={}

for tag in tags:
    start_prob[tag]=starting_tag_count[tag]/tags_count[tag]

for tag_state in to_pass_states :
basic_model.add_transition(basic_model.start,tag_state,start_prob[tag_state
.name])

end_prob={}

for tag in tags:
    end_prob[tag]=ending_tag_count[tag]/tags_count[tag]
for tag_state in to_pass_states :
basic_model.add_transition(tag_state,basic_model.end,end_prob[tag_state.nam
e])

transition_prob_pair={}
```

```
for key in tag_bigrams.keys():
    transition_prob_pair[key]=tag_bigrams.get(key)/tags_count[key[0]]
for tag_state in to_pass_states :
    for next_tag_state in to_pass_states :
basic_model.add_transition(tag_state,next_tag_state,transition_prob_pair[(t
ag_state.name,next_tag_state.name)])


basic_model.bake()

>>> for key in data.testing_set.keys[:2]:
...     print("Sentence Key: {}\n".format(key))
...     print("Predicted labels:\n-----------------")
...     print(simplify_decoding(data.sentences[key].words, basic_model))
...     print()
...     print("Actual labels:\n--------------")
...     print(data.sentences[key].tags)
...     print("\n")
```

```
Sentence Key: b100-28144

Predicted labels:
----------------
['CONJ', 'NOUN', 'NUM', '.', 'NOUN', 'NUM', '.', 'NOUN', 'NUM', '.', 'CONJ', 'NOUN', 'NUM', '.', '.', 'NOUN', '.', '.']

Actual labels:
-------------
('CONJ', 'NOUN', 'NUM', '.', 'NOUN', 'NUM', '.', 'NOUN', 'NUM', '.', 'CONJ', 'NOUN', 'NUM', '.', '.', 'NOUN', '.', '.')


Sentence Key: b100-23146

Predicted labels:
----------------
['PRON', 'VERB', 'DET', 'NOUN', 'ADP', 'ADJ', 'ADJ', 'NOUN', 'VERB', 'VERB', '.', 'ADP', 'VERB', 'DET', 'NOUN', 'ADP', 'NOUN',
'ADP', 'DET', 'NOUN', '.']

Actual labels:
-------------
('PRON', 'VERB', 'DET', 'NOUN', 'ADP', 'ADJ', 'ADJ', 'NOUN', 'VERB', 'VERB', '.', 'ADP', 'VERB', 'DET', 'NOUN', 'ADP', 'NOUN',
'ADP', 'DET', 'NOUN', '.')
```

```
>>> hmm_training_acc = accuracy(data.training_set.X, data.training_set.Y,
basic_model)
>>> print("Training accuracy basic hmm model: {:.2f}%".format(100 *
hmm_training_acc))
Training accuracy basic hmm model: 97.49%

>>> hmm_testing_acc = accuracy(data.testing_set.X, data.testing_set.Y,
basic_model)
>>> print("Testing accuracy basic hmm model: {:.2f}%".format(100 *
hmm_testing_acc))
Testing accuracy basic hmm model: 96.09%
```

We can see that the HMM-based model has been able to improve the accuracy of our model.

Speech recognition

In the 1950s, Bell Labs was the pioneer in speech recognition. The early designed systems were limited to a single speaker and had a very limited vocabulary. After around 70 years of work, the current speech-recognition systems are able to work with speech from multiple speakers and can recognize thousands of words in multiple languages. A detailed discussion of all the techniques used is beyond the scope of this book as enough work has been done on each technique to have a book on itself.

But the general workflow for a speech-recognition system is to first capture the audio by converting the physical sound into an electrical signal using a microphone. The electrical signal generated by the microphone is analog and needs to be converted to a digital form for storage and processing, for which analog-to-digital converters are used. Once we have the speech in digital form, we can apply algorithms on it to understand the speech.

As mentioned before, most of the state-of-the-art speech-recognition systems still use the concept of **Hidden Markov Models** (**HMM**) as their core. This is based on the assumption that a speech signal is a stationary process in a short time period of a few milliseconds. Hence, the first step for the speech-recognition system is to split the signal into small fragments of around 10 milliseconds. Then the power spectrum of each fragment is mapped to a vector of real numbers, known as **cepstral coefficients**. The dimension of this vector is usually small, although more accurate systems usually work with more than 32 dimensions. The final output of the HMM model is a sequence of these vectors. Once we have these vectors, these groups of vectors are matched to one or more phonemes, which are a fundamental unit of speech. But for effectively matching these groups of vectors to phonemes, we need to train our system since there is a huge variation in the sound of phonemes between different speakers as well as different utterances from the same speaker. Once we have the sequence of phonemes, our system tries to guess the most likely word that could have possibly produced that sequence of phonemes.

As we can imagine, this whole detection process can be computationally quite expensive. For dealing with this complexity issue, modern speech-recognition systems use neural networks for feature-transformation and dimensionality-reduction before using the HMM for recognition. Another commonly used technique to reduce computation is to use voice activity detectors, which can detect the regions in the signal that contain speech. Using this information, we can design the recognizer to only spend computation on the parts of the signal that contain speech.

Fortunately, Python has a very developed ecosystem to work with speech recognition. In the next section, we will look into the different Python packages available for working with speech recognition.

Python packages for speech recognition

The Python package hosting service, PyPI, has a lot of speech-recognition systems listed. Some of the most commonly used ones are as follows:

- SpeechRecognition (https://pypi.org/project/SpeechRecognition/)
- apiai (https://pypi.org/project/apiai/)
- assemblyai (https://pypi.org/project/assemblyai/)
- pocketsphinx (https://pypi.org/project/pocketsphinx/)
- google-cloud-speech (https://pypi.org/project/google-cloud-speech/)
- watson-developer-cloud (https://pypi.org/project/watson-developer-cloud/)

Some of these Python packages (such as apiai) offer more than just speech recognition and have implementations of natural language processing algorithms, using which the user can identify the speaker's intent from speech. The other packages focus only on speech recognition, which can be used to convert audio to text.

In this chapter, we will use the SpeechRecognition package. We have chosen SpeechRecognition for two reasons:

- It has a very simple-to-use API to directly access and process audio signals. For other packages, we usually need to write small scripts for them to be able to access files.
- It is a wrapper over several popular speech APIs and therefore is extremely flexible, and multiple services can be used without making much change to our code.

So, to start using SpeechRecognition, we need to install the package. Since it's hosted on PyPI, it can be installed directly using pip:

```
pip install SpeechRecognition
```

Basics of SpeechRecognition

The most important class in the package is the `Recognizer` class as it handles most of the recognition tasks. We can specify different settings and functionality for recognizing speech from an audio source while initializing the class.

The `Recognizer` class can be initialized very easily without passing any argument:

```
>>> import speech_recognition as sr
>>> r = sr.Recognizer()
```

Each instance of the `Recognizer` class has seven different possible methods that can be used to convert speech to text. Each of these methods uses a specific speech-recognition service. The seven methods are the following:

- `recognize_bing`: Uses Microsoft's Bing Speech.
- `recognize_google`: Uses Google's Web Speech API.
- `recognize_google_cloud`: Uses Google's Cloud Speech. Using this method would need `google-cloud-speech` to be installed, which can be easily installed through `pip` by running `pip install google-cloud-speech`.
- `recognize_houndify`: Uses SoundHound's Houndify.
- `recognize_ibm`: Uses IBM's speech to text.
- `recognize_sphinx`: Uses CMU's Sphinx. This method has a dependency on `PocketSphinx`, which can be installed by running `pip install pocketsphinx`.
- `recognize_wit`: Uses Wit.ai.

One important thing to keep in mind while using these methods is that since most of these recognition services are offered by companies through web APIs, we need an internet connection to access these services. Also, some of these services only allow usage after registering with them online. Out of these seven, only `recognize_sphinx` works offline.

Out of all these web APIs, only Google's Web Speech API works without any registration or API key. Therefore, to keep things simple, we will use that in the rest of this chapter.

 The recognize methods throw `RequestError` if the server is unavailable, there is no internet connection, or the API quota limits are met.

The next thing that we would need in order to do any recognition is some audio data. `SpeechRecognition` provides direct functionality to either work with an audio file or use audio from an attached microphone. In the following sections, we will look into both of these methods.

Speech recognition from audio files

To start working with audio files, we first need to download one. For the following example, we will use the `harvard.wav` file, which can be downloaded from `https://raw.` `githubusercontent.com/realpython/python-speech-recognition/master/audio_files/` `harvard.wav`.

 Make sure to save the audio files in the same directory from where the Python interpreter is running. Otherwise, for the following code, the path to the files will need to be modified.

For working with audio files, `SpeechRecognition` has the `AudioFile` class, which can be used for reading and working with audio files. We can use the `record` method of `AudioFile` to process the contents of the audio file before it can be used with the `Recognizer` class:

```
>>> harvard = sr.AudioFile('harvard.wav')
>>> with harvard as source:
...     audio = r.record(source)
```

The context manager opens the audio and records its content into `audio`, which is an instance of `AudioFile`. We can check it by calling the `type` method on `audio`:

```
>>> type(audio)
<class 'speech_recognition.AudioData'>
```

Now, once we have an `AudioFile` instance, we can call any of the recognize methods with it as an argument. The recognize method would call the specific web API to translate the speech from the audio file and return the following text:

```
>>> r.recognize_google(audio)
'the stale smell of old beer lingers it takes heat
to bring out the odor a cold dip restores health and
zest a salt pickle taste fine with ham tacos al
Pastore are my favorite a zestful food is the hot
cross bun'
```

In this case, we transcribed the whole audio file, but what if we want to only translate a specific part of the audio file? This can be done by passing additional arguments to the `record` method:

```
>>> with harvard as source:
...     audio_part = r.record(source, duration=4)

>>> r.recognize_google(audio_part)
'the stale smell of old beer lingers'
```

 The `record` method keeps a pointer in the audio file to point at the position until which recording has happened. So, if we do another record of four seconds on the same file, it will record from the four-second mark to the eight-second mark of the original audio file.

In the preceding example, we transcribed a part of the audio file but the starting point was the start of the file. What if we want to start at a different time point? It can be done by passing another argument, `offset`, to the `record` method:

```
>>> with harvard as source:
...     audio_offset = r.record(source, offset=4, duration=3)

>>> recognizer.recognize_google(audio_offset)
'it takes heat to bring out the odor'
```

If you listen to the `harvard.wav` file, you will realize that the recording is done in perfect conditions without any external noise, but that is usually not the case in real-life audio. Let's try to transcribe another audio signal, `jackhammer.wav`, which can be downloaded from https://raw.githubusercontent.com/realpython/python-speech-recognition/ master/audio_files/jackhammer.wav. If you listen to the audio file, you can notice that it has a lot of background noise. Let's try to transcribe this file and see how the recognizer performs:

```
>>> jackhammer = sr.AudioFile('jackhammer.wav')
>>> with jackhammer as source:
...     audio_jack = r.record(source)

>>> r.recognize_google(audio_jack)
'the snail smell of old gear vendors'
```

As we can see, the transcription is way off. In such cases, we can use the `adjust_for_ambient_noise` method provided in the `Recognizer` class to calibrate our audio signal with the noise.

`adjust_for_ambient_noise` by default uses the first one second of data to do the calibration, but we can change that by passing a `duration` argument to it:

```
>>> with jackhammer as source:
...         r.adjust_for_ambient_noise(source, duration=1)
...         audio = r.record(source)

>>> r.recognize_google(audio)
'still smell of old beer vendors'
```

If we don't want to lose much information, we can reduce the value of the `duration` argument, but that can result in a poorer calibration. As we can see, the transcription is still not perfect, but it is much better than when we didn't use `adjust_for_ambient_noise`. We can actually get better results by trying to clean the noise from the audio using signal processing techniques, which are outside the scope of this book.

Another thing that we can do in such cases is to look at all the most likely transcriptions by the recognizer. It can be done by using the `show_all` argument while calling the `recognize` method:

```
>>> r.recognize_google(audio, show_all=True)
{'alternative': [
  {'transcript': 'the snail smell like old Beer Mongers'},
  {'transcript': 'the still smell of old beer vendors'},
  {'transcript': 'the snail smell like old beer vendors'},
  {'transcript': 'the stale smell of old beer vendors'},
  {'transcript': 'the snail smell like old beermongers'},
  {'transcript': 'destihl smell of old beer vendors'},
  {'transcript': 'the still smell like old beer vendors'},
  {'transcript': 'bastille smell of old beer vendors'},
  {'transcript': 'the still smell like old beermongers'},
  {'transcript': 'the still smell of old beer venders'},
  {'transcript': 'the still smelling old beer vendors'},
  {'transcript': 'musty smell of old beer vendors'},
  {'transcript': 'the still smell of old beer vendor'}
], 'final': True}
```

Using this, we can then choose the best transcription for our specific problem.

Speech recognition using the microphone

In the previous section, we used the recognizer methods to transcribe speech from audio files. In this section, we will do a transcription using speech recorded from our microphone.

But before we get into that, we will need to install an additional package, called PyAudio. It is also available on PyPI and can be installed directly using pip: pip install PyAudio.

In the previous section, for working with audio files, we were using the AudioFile class, but for working with a microphone, we will need to use the Microphone class. Most of the recognition API still remains the same. Let's take a simple example to understand how it works:

```
>>> import speech_recognition as sr
>>> r = sr.Recognizer()

>>> mic = sr.Microphone()

>>> with mic as source:
...     r.adjust_for_ambient_noise(source)
...     audio = r.listen(source)
```

Similarly to how we had initialized the AudioFile class in the previous section, we need to initialize the Microphone class this time. Also, instead of record, we need to call the listen method to record the audio. The Python interpreter would wait for a while to record audio when executing the previous code block. Try saying something into the microphone. Once the interpreter prompt returns, we can call the recognize method to transcribe the recorded audio:

```
>>> r.recognize_google(audio)
'hello world' # This would depend on what you said in the microphone
```

Summary

In this chapter, we looked into two of the major applications of HMMs: POS tagging and speech recognition. We coded the POS tagger using a most-frequent tag algorithm and used the pomegranate package to build one based on HMM. We compared the performance using both these methods and saw that an HMM-based approach outperforms the most-frequent tag method. Then, we used the SpeechRecognition package to transcribe audio to text using Google's Web Speech API. We looked into using the package with both audio files and live audio from a microphone.

In the next chapter, we will explore more applications of HMMs, specifically in the field of image recognition.

8
2D HMM for Image Processing

In this chapter, we will introduce the application of HMM in the case of image segmentation. For image segmentation, we usually split up the given image into multiple blocks of equal size and then perform an estimation for each of these blocks. However, these algorithms usually ignore the contextual information from the neighboring blocks. To deal with that issue, 2D HMMs were introduced, which consider feature vectors to be dependent through an underlying 2D Markovian mesh. In this chapter, we will discuss how these 2D HMMs work and will derive parameter estimation algorithms for them. In this chapter, we will discuss the following topics:

- Pseudo 2D HMMs
- Introduction to 2D HMMs
- Parameter learning in 2D HMMs
- Applications

Recap of 1D HMM

Let's recap how 1D HMMs work, which we discussed in the previous chapters of this book. We have seen that HMM is a just a process over Markov chains. At any point in time, an HMM is in one of the possible states, and the next state that the model will transition to depends on the current state and the transition probability of the model.

Suppose that there are $M = \{1, 2, ..., M\}$ possible states for HMM, and the transition probability of going from some state i to state j is given by $a_{i,j}$. For such a model, if at time $t\text{-}1$ the model is at state i, then at time t it would be in state j with a probability of $a_{i,j}$. This probability is known as the **transition probability**. Also, we have defined the observed variable in the model, which only depends on the current state of our hidden variable. We can define the observed variable at time t as u_t, so let's say the emission distribution for the state i for the variable u_t is given by $b_i(u_t)$.

We also need to define the initial probability, π_i, as the probability of being in state i at time $t = 1$. With all these given values, we can determine the likelihood of observing any given sequence, $\mathbf{u} = \{u_t\}_{t=1}^T$, as follows:

$$P(\mathbf{u}) = \sum_{s_1,s_2,\ldots,s_u} \pi_{s_1} b_{s_1}(u_1) a_{s_1,s_2} b_{s_2}(u_2)\ldots a_{s_{T-1},s_T} b_{s_T}(u_T)$$

In most situations, we assume the states to be a Gaussian mixture model; in which case, the previous equation can be generalized further, as follows:

$$b_i(u_t) = \frac{1}{\sqrt{(2\pi)^k \det(\Sigma_i)}} \exp^{-\frac{1}{2}(u_t - u_i)^t \Sigma_i^{-1}(u_t - u_i)}$$

Here, u_i is the mean, Σ_i is the covariance matrix, and k is the dimensionality of the observed variable u_t.

Now we have our model defined, we can move on to the estimation method. Estimation is usually performed using the Baum-Welch algorithm that we saw in Chapter 4, *Parameter Inference using Maximum Likelihood*, which performs a maximum-likelihood estimation. Let $L_i(t)$ be the conditional distribution of being in state i at time t, given the observations, and $H_{i,j}(t)$ be the conditional probability of transitioning to state j from state i at time $t + 1$, again, given the observations. Then, we can re-estimate the mean, covariance, and transition probability as follows:

$$\hat{\mu}_i = \frac{\sum_{t=1}^T L_i(t) u_t}{\sum_{t=1}^T L_i(t)}$$

$$\hat{\Sigma}_i = \frac{\sum_{t=1}^T L_i(t)(u_t - \hat{\mu}_i)(u_t - \hat{\mu}_i)^t}{\sum_{t=1}^T L_i(t)}$$

$$\hat{a}_{i,j} = \frac{\sum_{t=1}^{T-1} H_{i,j}(t)}{\sum_{t=1}^T L_i(t)}$$

To compute the values of $L_i(t)$ and $H_{i,j}(t)$, we use the forward-backward algorithm. The forward algorithm gives us the probability, $\alpha_i(t)$, of observing the first t outcomes, $\{u_\tau\}_{\tau=1,2,\ldots,t}$, and being in state i at time t.

This probability can be evaluated using the following set of equations:

$$\alpha_i(1) = \pi_i b_i(u_i) \quad 1 \leq i \leq M$$

$$\alpha_i(t) = b_i(u_t) \sum_{j=1}^{M} \alpha_j(t-1)a_{j,i} \quad 1 < t \leq T, 1 \leq i \leq M$$

We also define the backward probability, $\beta_i(t)$, as the conditional probability of having the observations $\{u_r\}r=t+1,...,T$, given that the model is in state i at time t. The conditional probability $\beta_i(t)$ can be computed as follows:

$$\beta_i(T) = 1$$

$$\beta_i(t) = \sum_{j=1}^{M} a_{i,j} b_j(u_{t+1}) \beta_j(t+1) \quad 1 \leq t \leq T$$

With these values to hand, we can compute that $L_i(t)$ and $H_{i,j}(t)$ can be solved as follows:

$$L_i(t) = P(s_t = i|\mathbf{u}) = \frac{P(\mathbf{u}, s_t = i)}{P(\mathbf{u})}$$

$$= \frac{1}{P(\mathbf{u})} \alpha_i(t)\beta_i(t)$$

$$H_{i,j}(t) = P(s_t = i, s_{t+1} = j|u)$$

$$= \frac{1}{P(\mathbf{u})} \alpha_i(t)a_{i,j}b_j(u_{t+1})\beta_j(t+1)$$

We can approximate this algorithm by assuming each observation to have resulted from the most likely hidden state. This allows us to simplify the Baum-Welch algorithm; this is commonly also known as the **Viterbi training algorithm**. Given the observed states, and assuming the state sequence to be $\mathbf{s} = \{s_t\}_{t=1}^{T}$ with the maximum conditional probability, this can be given as follows:

$$\mathbf{s}^* = \max_{\mathbf{s}}^{-1} P(\mathbf{s}|\mathbf{u}) = \max_{\mathbf{s}}^{-1} P(\mathbf{s}, \mathbf{u})$$

Here, $\underset{\mathbf{s}}{\max} P(\mathbf{s}, \mathbf{u})$ can be computed as follows:

$$\theta_i(1) = \pi_i b_i(u_i) \quad 1 \leq i \leq M$$
$$\theta_i(t) = \max_j \{\theta_j(t-1)a_{j,i}\} b_i(u_t) \quad 1 < i \leq T, 1 \leq i \leq M$$
$$\max_{\mathbf{s}} P(\mathbf{s}, \mathbf{u}) = \max_j \theta_j(T)$$

With these values, we can then compute the model parameters as follows:

$$\hat{\mu}_i = \frac{\sum_{t=1}^{T} I(s_t^* = i) u_t}{\sum_{t=1}^{T} I(s_t^* = i)}$$

$$\hat{\Sigma}^i = \frac{\sum_{t=1}^{T} I(s_t^*)(u_t - \hat{\mu}_i)(u_t - \hat{\mu}_i)^t}{\sum_{t=1}^{T} I(s_t^* = i)}$$

$$\hat{a}_{i,j} = \frac{\sum_{t=1}^{T-1} I(s_t^* = i) I(s_{t+1}^* = j)}{\sum_{t=1}^{T} I(s_t^* = i)}$$

Here, I is the indicator function, which returns 1 if the function's argument is true; otherwise, it returns 0.

In this section, we have quickly reviewed the basic concepts of 1D HMMs when the states are parameterized using Gaussian mixture models, so we can now move on to 2D HMMs.

2D HMMs

A lot of work has been done regarding 2D HMMs, but the most recent work and well-received work has been done by Jia Li, Amir Najmi, and Robert Gray in their paper, *Image Classification by a Two Dimensional Hidden Markov Model*. This section has been written based on their work. We will start by giving the general algorithm they have introduced, and then, in further subsections, we will see how the algorithm works.

Algorithm

The algorithm for image classification is as follows:

- Training:
  - Divide the training images into non-overlapping blocks with equal size and extract a feature vector for each block
  - Select the number of states for the 2D HMM
  - Estimate the model parameters based on the feature vectors and the training labels

- Testing:
  - Similar to training, generate feature vectors for the testing images
  - Search for the set of classes with the maximum a posteriori probability, given the feature vectors, according to the training model

Assumptions for the 2D HMM model

In this section, we will quickly go through the assumptions for the 2D HMM model and the derivation of how these assumptions simplify our equations. For a more detailed derivation, please refer to the original paper.

We start by dividing the image into smaller blocks, from which we evaluate the feature vectors, and, using these feature vectors, we classify the image. In the case of a 2D HMM, we make the assumption that the feature vectors are generated by a Markov model with a state change happening once every block. We also define the relationship between the blocks based on which block comes before or after which block. A block at position (i', j') is said to come before the block at position (i, j) if i' or $i' = i$ and $j' < j$. Assuming that there are $M = \{1, 2, ... M\}$ states, the state of any given block at position (i, j) is denoted by $S_{i,j}$, the feature vector is denoted by $u_{i,j}$ and the class is denoted by $c_{i,j}$. Another point to keep in mind is that the order of the blocks has been introduced just to explain the assumptions of the model, and the algorithm doesn't consider any order of blocks while doing the classification.

The first assumption made by the model is as follows:

$$P(s_{i,j}|s_{i',j'}, u_{i',j'} : (i',j') \in \Psi) = a_{m,n,l},$$
$$where\ \Psi = \{(i',j') : (i',j') < (i,j)\}$$
$$and\ m = s_{i-1,j}, n = s_{i,j-1},\ and\ l = s_{i,j}$$

This assumption states that knowing the current state is a sufficient statistic for estimating the transition probabilities, which means that u is conditionally independent. Also, according to the assumption, the state transition is a Markov process in two dimensions, and the probability of the system entering any particular state depends on the state of the model in both the horizontal and vertical directions in the previous time and observation instance. We also assume that there is one-to-one mapping from state to class, so that once we know the state, the class can be directly computed.

The second assumption is that the feature vectors are a Gaussian mixture distribution for each state. We know that any M-component Gaussian mixture can be split into M substates with single Gaussian distributions; therefore, for a block with state s and feature vector u, the probability of the distribution is given by the following:

$$b_s(u) = \frac{1}{\sqrt{(2\pi)^k |\Sigma_s|}} \exp^{-\frac{1}{2}(u-\mu_s)^t \Sigma_s^{-1}(u-\mu_s)}$$

Here, Σ_s is the covariance matrix and μ_s is the mean vector of the Gaussian distribution.

We can now use the Markovian assumptions to simplify the evaluation of the probability of the states. The probability of the states for all the blocks in the image is denoted by $P\{s_{i,j} : (i,j) \in N\}$, where $N = \{(i,j) : 0 \leq i < w, 0 \leq j < z\}$. But before we use the Markovian assumptions to efficiently expand the probability, we need to prove that, given the two previous assumptions, a rotated form of two-dimensional Markovian property holds for the image.

We define a rotated relation of "$<$", denoted by "$\hat{<}$", which specifies $(i',j') \hat{<} (i,j)$, if $j' < j$, or $j' = j$ and $i' < i$. We need to prove the following:

$$P(s_{i,j} | s_{i',j'}, u_{i',j'} : (i',j') \in \hat{\Psi}) = a_{m,n,l},$$
$$\text{where } \hat{\Psi} = \{(i',j') : (i',j') \hat{<} (i,j)\}$$
$$\text{and } m = s_{i-1,j}, n = s_{i,j-1}, \text{ and } l = s_{i,j}$$

So, we use the previous definition of $\Psi = \{(i',j') : (i',j') < (i,j)\}$ and introduce the following new notation:

$$\hat{\Psi} \cup \Psi = \{(i',j') : (i',j') < (i,j) \text{ or } (i',j') \hat{<} (i,j)\},$$
$$\hat{\Psi} \cap \Psi = \{(i',j') : (i',j') < (i,j) \text{ and } (i',j') \hat{<} (i,j)\},$$
$$\hat{\Psi} - \Psi = \{(i',j') : (i',j') \hat{<} (i,j) \text{ and } (i',j') > (i,j)\}$$

From the preceding equations, we can also see this:

$$\hat{\Psi} = (\hat{\Psi} \cap \Psi) \cup (\hat{\Psi} - \Psi)$$

Now, to simplify notation, let's introduce $\gamma_0 = P(s_{i',j'}, u_{i',j'} : (i',j') \in \hat{\Psi})$ and $\gamma_1 = P(s_{i',j'}, u_{i',j'} : (i',j') \in \hat{\Psi} \cap \Psi)$. From these we can do the following derivation:

$$P(s_{i,j} | s_{i',j'}, u_{i',j'} : (i',j') \in \hat{\Psi})$$

$$= \frac{1}{\gamma_0} \cdot P(s_{i,j}, s_{i',j'}, u_{i',j'}, s_{i'',j''}, u_{i'',j''} : (i',j') \in \hat{\Psi} \cap \Psi, (i'',j'') \in \hat{\Psi} - \Psi$$

Expanding the conditional probability, we get the following:

$$= \frac{\gamma_1}{\gamma_0} P(s_{i,j} | s_{i',j'}, u_{i',j'} : (i',j') \in \hat{\Psi} \cap \Psi).$$
$$P(s_{i'',j''}, u_{i'',j''} : (i'',j'') \in \hat{\Psi} - \Psi | s_{i,j}, s_{i',j'}, u_{i',j'} : (i',j') \in \hat{\Psi} \cap \Psi)$$

Using the Markovian assumption, we get the following:

$$= \frac{\gamma_1}{\gamma_0} \cdot P(s_{i,j} | s_{i-1,j}, s_{i,j-1}).$$
$$P(s_{i'',j''}, u_{i'',j''} : (i'',j'') \in \hat{\Psi} - \Psi | s_{i,j}, s_{i',j'}, u_{i',j'} : (i',j') \in \hat{\Psi} \cap \Psi)$$

And, finally, using the Markovian assumption and the assumption that the feature vector of a block is conditionally independent of other blocks given its state, we have the following:

$$= P(s_{i,j} | s_{i-1,j}, s_{i,j-1}).$$
$$\frac{\gamma_1}{\gamma_0} \cdot P(s_{i'',j''}, u_{i'',j''} : (i'',j'') \in \hat{\Psi} - \Psi | s_{i',j'}, ui', j' : (i',j') \in \hat{\Psi} \cap \Psi)$$
$$= P(s_{i,j} | s_{i-1,j} s_{i,j-1})$$
$$= a_{m,n,l}$$

Where $m = s_{i-1,j}$, $n = s_{i,j-1}$, and $l = s_{i,j}$.

If we replace $\hat{\Psi} \cap \Psi$ with Ψ, and replace $\hat{\Psi}$ with $\hat{\Psi} \cup \Psi$ in the derivation, all the equations will still hold. This gives us the following:

$$P(s_{i,j}|s_{i',j'}, u_{i',j'}) : (i', j') \in \hat{\Psi} \cup \Psi) = P(s_{i,j}|s_{i-1,j}, s_{i,j-1})$$

Since the preceding equation implies the original Markovian assumption and its rotated version, we can show the equivalent end of the two assumptions as follows:

$$P(s_{i,j}|s_{i',j'}, u_{i',j'} : (i', j') \in \Psi) = P(s_{i,j}|s_{i-1,j}, s_{i,j-1}) \ and$$
$$P(s_{i,j}|s_{i',j'}, u_{i',j'} : (i', j') \in \hat{\Psi} \cup \Psi) = P(s_{i,j}|s_{i-1,j}, s_{i,j-1})$$

Now we can simplify the expansion of $P\{s_{i,j} : (i,j) \in N\}$, as follows:

$$P\{s_{i,j} : (i, j) \in \mathcal{N}\} = P(T_0).\, P(T_1|T_0)\ldots P(T_{w+z-2}|T_{w+z-3}, T_{w+z-4}, \ldots, T_0)$$

Here, w and z are the numbers of rows and columns in the image, respectively, and T_i is the sequence of states for blocks on the diagonal i. Next, we need to prove that $P(T_i|T_{i-1},...,T_0) = P(T_i|T_{i-1})$. Assuming $T_i = \{s_{i,0}, s_{i-1,1}, ..., s_{0,i}\}$, this means $T_{i-1} = \{s_{i-1,0}, s_{i-2,1}, ..., s_{0,i-1}\}$ and hence we have the following:

$$\begin{aligned} P(T_i|T_{i-1}, \ldots, T_0) &= P(s_{i,0}, s_{i-1,1}, \ldots, s_{0,i}|T_{i-1}, T_{i-1}, \ldots, T_0) \\ &= P(s_{i,0}|T_{i-1}, \ldots, T_0).\, P(s_{i-1,1}|s_{i,0}, T_{i-1}, \ldots, T_0) \\ &\quad \ldots P(s_{0,i}|s_{1,i-1}, \ldots, s_{i,0}, T_{i-1}, \ldots, T_0) \\ &= P(s_{i,0}|s_{i-1,0}).\, P(s_{i-1,1}|s_{i-2,1}, s_{i-2,1}, s_{i-1,0}) \ldots P(s_{0,i}|s_{0,i-1}) \end{aligned}$$

Therefore, we can conclude:

$$P(T_i|T_{i-1}, \ldots, T_0) = P(T_i|T_{i-1})$$

Using this, we get the following simplified equation:

$$P\{s_{i,j} : (i, j) \in \mathcal{N}\} = P(T_0).\, P(T_1|T_0)\ldots P(T_{w+z-2}|T_{w+z-3})$$

Parameter estimation using EM

Since we have the model ready, we now need to estimate the parameters of the model. We need to estimate the mean vectors μ_m; the covariance matrices Σ_m; and the transition probabilities $a_{m,n,l}$, where $m,n,l = 1,..., M$, and M is the total number of states. We will use the **expectation maximization** (**EM**) algorithm.

As we have seen in previous chapters, EM is an iterative algorithm that can learn the maximum likelihood estimates in the case of missing data; that is, when we have unobserved variables in our data. Let's say that our unobserved variable x is in the sample space x, and the observed variable y *is* in the sample space y. If we postulate a family of distribution $f(x | \Phi)$, with parameters $\Phi \in \Omega$, then the distribution over y is given as follows:

$$g(\mathbf{y}|\phi) = \int_{\chi(\mathbf{y})} f(\mathbf{x}|\phi)d\mathbf{x}$$

The EM algorithm will then try to find the value of ϕ that would maximize the value of $g(y | \Phi)$ given the observed y. The EM iteration $\Phi^{(p)} \to \Phi^{(p+1)}$ is defined as follows:

- **E-step**: Compute $Q(\Phi | \Phi^{(p)})$ where $Q(\Phi' | \Phi)$ is the expected value of $log\, f(x | \Phi')$
- **M-step**: Choose $\Phi^{(p+1)}$ to be a value of $\Phi \in \Omega$ that maximizes $Q(\Phi | \Phi^{(p)})$

Let's now define the terms needed for 2D HMMs:

- The set of observed feature vectors for the entire image is $\mathbf{u} = \{u_{i,j} : (i,j) \in \mathcal{N}\}$
- The set of states for the image is $\mathbf{s} = \{s_{i,j} : (i,j) \in \mathcal{N}\}$
- The set of classes for the image is $\mathbf{c} = \{c_{i,j} : (i,j) \in \mathcal{N}\}$
- The mapping from a state $s_{i,j}$ to its class is $C(s_{i,j})$, and the set of classes mapped from states s, is denoted by $C(s)$

Now let's define the distribution over x for a 2D HMM, as follows:

$$
\begin{aligned}
f(\mathbf{x}|\phi') &= P(\mathbf{s}|\phi').\,P(\mathbf{u}|\mathbf{s},\phi') \\
&= P(\mathbf{s}|a'_{m,n,l} : m,n,l \in \mathcal{M}).\,P(\mathbf{u}|\mathbf{s},\mu'_m, \Sigma'_m : m \in \mathcal{M}) \\
&= \prod_{(i,j)\in\mathcal{N}} a'_{s_{i-1,j},s_{i,j-1},s_{i,j}} \cdot \prod_{(i,j)\in\mathcal{N}} P(u_{i,j}|\mu'_{s_{i,j}}, \Sigma'_{s_{i,j}}).
\end{aligned}
$$

From this, we can compute the following $\log f(x \mid \Phi')$:

$$\log f(\mathbf{x}|\phi') = \sum_{(i,j)\in\mathcal{N}} \log a'_{s_{i-1,j},s_{i,j-1},s_{i,j}} + \sum_{(i,j)\in\mathcal{N}} \log P(u_{i,j}|\mu'_{s_{i,j}}, \Sigma'_{s_{i,j}}).$$

We now know that, given y, x can only have a finite number of values corresponding to states that are consistent with the value of y. Therefore, the distribution over x is given as follows:

$$P(\mathbf{x}|\mathbf{y}, \phi^{(p)}) = \frac{1}{\alpha} I(C(\mathbf{s}) = \mathbf{c}). P(\mathbf{s}|\phi^{(p)}). P(\mathbf{u}|\mathbf{s}, \phi^{(p)})$$

$$= \frac{1}{\alpha} I(C(\mathbf{s}) = \mathbf{c}). \prod_{(i,j)\in\mathcal{N}} a^{(p)}_{s_{i-1,j},s_{i,j-1},s_{i,j}} \cdot \prod_{(i,j)\in\mathcal{N}} P(u_{i,j}|\mu^{(p)}_{s_{i,j}}, \Sigma^{(p)}_{s_{i,j}})$$

Here, α is the normalizing constant and I is the indicator function. Now, for the M-step, we need to set the value of $\Phi^{(p+1)}$ to Φ', which will maximize the following:

$$E(\log f(\mathbf{x}|\phi')|\mathbf{y}, \phi^{(p)}) = \frac{1}{\alpha} \sum_{\mathbf{s}} P(\mathbf{s}|\mathbf{y}, \phi^{(p)}). \sum_{(i,j)\in\mathcal{N}} \log a'_{s_{i-1,j},s_{i,j-1},s_{i,j}} +$$

$$\frac{1}{\alpha} \sum_{\mathbf{s}} P(\mathbf{s}|\mathbf{y}, \phi^{(p)}) \sum_{(i,j)\in\mathcal{N}} \log P(u_{i,j}|\mu'_{s_{i,j}}, \Sigma'_{s_{i,j}})$$

Since the previous term has two parts with an addition between them, we can deal with each term separately, since we are trying to maximize the total. Consider the first term:

$$\sum_{\mathbf{s}} P(\mathbf{s}|\mathbf{y}, \phi^{(p)}). \sum_{(i,j)\in\mathcal{N}} \log a'_{s_{i-1,j},s_{i,j-1},s_{i,j}}$$

$$= \sum_{\mathbf{s}} P(\mathbf{s}|\mathbf{y}, \phi^{(p)}) l \sum_{m,n,l\in\mathcal{M}} \sum_{(i,j)\in\mathcal{N}} \log a'_{m,n,l}. I(m = s_{i-1,j}, n = s_{i,j-1}, l = s_{i,j})$$

$$= \sum_{m,n,l\in\mathcal{M}} \log a'_{m,n,l} \sum_{(i,j)\in\mathcal{N}} \sum_{\mathbf{s}} P(\mathbf{s}|\mathbf{y}, \phi^{(p)}) I(m = s_{i-1,j}, n = s_{i,j-1}, l = s_{i,j})$$

By defining $H^{(p)}_{m,n,l}(i,j) = \sum_{\mathbf{s}} I(m = s_{i-1,j}, n = s_{i,j-1}, l = s_{i,j}) P(\mathbf{s}|\mathbf{y}, \phi^{(\phi)})$, the preceding equation can be reduced to this:

$$\sum_{m,n,l\in\mathcal{M}} \log a'_{m,n,l} \sum_{(i,j)\in\mathcal{N}} H^{(p)}_{m,n,l}(i,j)$$

This term is concave in $a'_{m,n,l}$; therefore, using the Lagrangian multiplier and taking the derivative we get the following:

$$a'_{m,n,l} = \frac{\sum_{(i,j)\in\mathcal{N}} H^{(p)}_{m,n,l}(i,j)}{\sum_{l'=1}^{M} \sum_{(i,j)\in\mathcal{N}} H^{(p)}_{m,n,l'}(i,j)}$$

Coming back to maximizing the second term of $E(\log f(\mathbf{x}|\phi')|\mathbf{y},\phi^{(p)})$:

$$\sum_{\mathbf{s}} P(\mathbf{s}|\mathbf{y},\phi^{(p)}). \sum_{(i,j)\in\mathcal{N}} \log P(u_{i,j}|\mu'_{s_{i,j}}, \Sigma'_{s_{i,j}})$$

$$= \sum_{\mathbf{s}} P(\mathbf{s}|\mathbf{y},\phi^{(p)}). \sum_{m=1}^{M} \sum_{(i,j)\in\mathcal{N}} \log P(u_{i,j}|\mu'_m, \Sigma'_m) I(m = s_{i,j})$$

$$= \sum_{m=1}^{M} \sum_{(i,j)\in\mathcal{N}} \sum_{\mathbf{s}} I(m = s_{i,j}) P(\mathbf{s}|\mathbf{y},\phi^{(p)}). \log P(u_{i,j}|\mu'_m, \Sigma'_m)$$

Again, to simplify the preceding equation, we define $L^{(p)}_m(i,j) = \sum_{\mathbf{s}} I(m = s_{i,j}) P(\mathbf{s}|\mathbf{y},\phi^{(p)})$, and the preceding term becomes this:

$$\sum_{m=1}^{M} \sum_{(i,j)\in\mathcal{N}} L^{(p)}_m(i,j) \log P(u_{i,j}|\mu'_m, \Sigma'_m)$$

In this case, our ML estimates for our Gaussian distribution are given by the following:

$$\mu'_m = \frac{\sum_{i,j} L^{(p)}_m(i,j) u_{i,j}}{\sum_{i,j} L^{(p)}_m(i,j)}$$

$$\Sigma'_m = \frac{\sum_{i,j} L^{(p)}_m(i,j)(u_{i,j} - \mu'_m)(u_{i,j} - \mu'_m)^t}{\sum_{i,j} L^{(p)}_m(i,j)}$$

To summarize the whole derivation, we can write the EM algorithm in the following two steps:

1. Given the model estimation $\Phi^{(p)}$, the parameters are updated as follows:

$$\mu_m^{(p+1)} = \frac{\sum_{i,j} L_m^{(p)}(i,j) u_{i,j}}{\sum_{i,j} L_m^{(p)}(i,j)}$$

$$\Sigma_m^{(p+1)} = \frac{\sum_{i,j} L_m^{(p)}(i,j)(u_{i,j} - \mu_m^{(p+1)})(u_{i,j} - \mu_m^{(p+1)})^t}{\sum_{i,j} L_m^{(p)}(i,j)}$$

Here, the term $L_m^{(p)}(i,j)$ can be computed as this:

$$L_m^{(p)} = \sum_{s} I(m = s_{i,j}) . \frac{1}{\alpha} I(C(\mathbf{s}) = \mathbf{c}).$$

$$\prod_{(i',j') \in \mathcal{N}} a_{s_{i'-1,j}, s_{i',j'-1}, s_{i',j'}}^{(p)} . \prod_{(i',j') \in \mathcal{N}} P(u_{i',j'} | \mu_{s_{i',j'}}^{(p)}, \Sigma_{s_{i',j'}}^{(p)})$$

2. The transition probability is updated as follows:

$$a_{m,n,l}^{(p+1)} = \frac{\sum_{i,j} H_{m,n,l}^{(p)}(i,j)}{\sum_{l'=1}^{M} \sum_{i,j} H_{m,n,l'}^{(p)}(i,j)}$$

And, here, $H_{m,n,l}^{(p)}(i,j)$ is calculated as follows:

$$H_{m,n,l}^{(p)}(i,j) = \sum_{s} I(m = s_{i-1,j}, n = s_{i,j-1}, l = s_{i,j}) . \frac{1}{\alpha} I(C(\mathbf{s}) = \mathbf{c})$$

$$\prod_{i',j' \in \mathcal{N}} a_{s_{i'-1,j}, s_{i',j'-1}, s_{i',j'}}^{(p)} . \prod_{(i',j') \in \mathcal{N}} P(u_{i',j'} | \mu_{s_{i',j'}}^{(p)}, \Sigma_{s_{i',j'}}^{(p)})$$

By applying the preceding two equations iteratively, our algorithm will converge to the maximum likelihood estimation of the parameters of the model.

Summary

In this chapter we started with a short recap of 1D HMMs which we introduced in the previous chapter. Later we introduced the concepts of 2D HMMs and derived the various assumptions that we make for 2D HMMs to simplify our computations and it can be applied in image processing tasks. We then introduce a generic EM algorithm for learning the parameters in the case of 2D-HMMs.

In the next chapter, we will look at another application of HMMs in the field of reinforcement learning and will introduce MDP.

9
Markov Decision Process

In this chapter, we will talk about another application of HMMs known as **Markov Decision Process** (**MDP**). In the case of MDPs, we introduce a reward to our model, and any sequence of states taken by the process results in a specific reward. We will also introduce the concept of discounts, which will allow us to control how short-sighted or far-sighted we want our agent to be. The goal of the agent would be to maximize the total reward that it can get.

In this chapter, we will be covering the following topics:

- Reinforcement learning
- The Markov reward process
- Markov decision processes
- Code example

Reinforcement learning

Reinforcement learning is a different paradigm in machine learning where an agent tries to learn to behave optimally in a defined environment by making decisions/actions and observing the outcome of that decision. So, in the case of reinforcement learning, the agent is not really from some given dataset, but rather, by interacting with the environment, the agent tries to learn by observing the effects of its actions. The environment is defined in such a way that the agent gets rewards if its action gets it closer to the goal.

Humans are known to learn in this way. For example, consider a child in front of a fireplace where the child is the agent and the space around the child is the environment. Now, if the child moves its hand towards the fire, it feels the warmth, which feels good and, in a way, the child (or the agent) is rewarded for the action of moving its hand close to the fire. But if the child moves its hand too close to the fire, its hand will burn, hence receiving a negative reward. Using these rewards, the child is able to figure out the optimal distance to keep its hand from the fire. Reinforcement learning tries to imitate exactly this kind of system in order to train the agent to learn to optimize its goal in the given environment.

Making this more formal, to train an agent we will need to have an environment which represents the world in which the agent should be able to take actions. For each of these actions, the environment should return observations which contain information about the reward, telling it how good or bad the action was. The observation should also have information regarding the next state of the agent in the environment. And, based on these observations, the agent tries to figure out the optimal way to reach its goal. *Figure 1* shows the interaction between an agent and an environment:

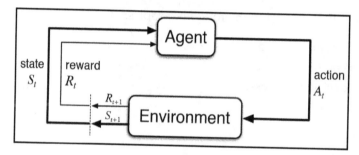

The thing that makes reinforcement learning fundamentally different from other algorithms is that there is no supervisor. Instead, there is only a reward signal giving feedback to the agent about the action it took. Another important thing to mention here is that an environment can be constructed in such a way that the reward is delayed, which can make the agent wander around before reaching its goal. It is also possible that the agent might have to go through a lot of negative feedback before reaching its goal.

In the case of supervised learning, we are given the dataset, which basically tells our learning algorithm the right answers in different situations. Our learning algorithm then looks over all these different situations, and the solutions in those cases, and tries to generalize based upon it. Hence, we also expect that the dataset given to use is **independent and identically distributed** (**IID**). But in the case of reinforcement learning the data is not IID, the data generated depends on the path the agent took, and, hence, it depends on the actions taken by the agent. Hence, reinforcement learning is an active learning process in which the actions taken by the agent influence the environment which in turn influences the data generated by the environment.

We can take a very simple example to better understand how a reinforcement learning agent and environment behave. Consider an agent trying to learn to play Super Mario Bros:

1. The agent will receive the initial state from the environment. In the case of Super Mario, this would be the current frame of the game.
2. Having received the state information, the agent will try to take an action. Let's say the action the agent took is to move to the right.
3. When the environment receives this action it will return the next state based on it. The next state would also be a frame, but the frame could be of a dying Mario if there was an enemy next to Mario in the previous state. Otherwise, the frame would just have shown Mario to have moved one step to the right. The environment will also return the rewards based on the action. If there was an enemy on the right of Mario the rewards could be, let's say -5 (since the action killed Mario) or could be +1 if the Mario moved towards finishing the level.

Reward hypothesis

The whole concept of reinforcement learning is based on something called **reward hypothesis**. According to reward hypothesis, all goals can be defined by the maximization of the expected cumulative reward.

At any given time t, the total cumulative reward can be given by:

$$G_t = R_{t+1} + R_{t+1} + \cdots$$

$$G_t = \sum_{k=0}^{T} R_{t+k+1}$$

But, in reality, the rewards which are closer to the current state are more probable that the ones which are further away. To deal with this, we would introduce another term called the **discount rate,** γ. The value of the discount rate is always between 0 and 1. A large value of γ means a smaller discount, which make the agent care more about the long-term rewards, whereas, for smaller values of γ, the agent cares more about the short-term rewards. With the discount rate term, we can now define our cumulative reward as:

$$G_t = \sum_{k=0}^{\infty} \gamma^k R_{t+k+1}$$

State of the environment and the agent

As we saw earlier, the agent interacts with the environment at intervals of time $t = 0, 1, 2, 3,$ .., and, at each time instance, the agent gets the state of the environment S_t based on which it takes an action A_t and gets a reward R_{t+1}. This sequence of state, action and rewards over time is known as the **history of the agent** and is given as:

$$H_t = S_1, A_1, R_2, \ldots, S_{t-1}, A_{t-1}, R_t$$

Ideally, we would like the action taken by the agent to be based on its total history, but it is generally unfeasible because the history of the agent can be huge. Therefore, we define the state in a way such that it is a summary of all the history of the agent:

$$S_t = f(H_t)$$

Basically, we are defining the state to be a function of the history of the agent. It's important to notice that the environment state is the state that the environment uses to determine its next state, based on the action, and give out rewards. Also, it is private to the environment.

On the other hand, the agent state is the state that the agent uses to decide on the next action. The agent state is its internal representation, and can be any function of the history as mentioned before.

We use a Markov state to represent an agent's state, which basically means that the current state of the agent is able to summarize all the history, and the next action of the agent will depend only on the current state of the agent. Hence,

$$P[S_{t+1} | S_t] = P[S_{t+1} | S_1, \ldots, S_t]$$

In this chapter, we will only be considering the case when the agent is directly able to observe the environment's state. This results in the observation from the environment to be both the current state of the agent as well as the environment. This special case is also commonly known as **MDP**.

Components of an agent

In this section, we will formally define the different kinds of components that an agent can have.

- **Policy**: It is a conditional over the action given the state. Based on this conditional distribution, the agent chooses its action at any given state. It is possible for the policy to be deterministic: $a = \pi(s)$ or stochastic: $\pi(a|s) = P[A_t = a|S_t = s]$.

- **Value function**: The value function tries to predict the reward to expect on taking a given action in a given state. It is given as:
  $v_\pi(s) = E_\pi[R_{t+1} + \gamma R_{t+2} + \gamma^2 R_{t+3} + \ldots | S_t = s]$.

  where E is the expectation and γ is the discount factor.

- **Model**: The model is the agent's representation of the environment. It is defined using a transition function P which predicts the next state of the environment:
  $\mathcal{P}_{ss'}^a = P[S_{t+1} = s'|S_t = s, A_t = a]$.

  and a reward function which predicts the reward associated with any given action at a given state: $\mathcal{R}_s^a = E[R_{t+1}|S_t = s, A_t = a]$.

Based on these components, agents can be classified into the following five categories:

- **Value-based agents**: Have an implicit policy and the agent takes decisions for actions based on the value function
- **Policy-based agents**: Have an explicit policy and the agent searches for the most optimal action-value function
- **Actor-critic agents**: Combination of both value-based and policy-based agents
- **Model-based agents**: Try to build a model based on the environment
- **Model-free agents**: Don't try to learn the environment, rather they try to learn the policy and value function

The Markov reward process

In the previous section, we gave an introduction to MDP. In this section, we will define the problem statement formally and see the algorithms for solving it.

An MDP is used to define the environment in reinforcement learning and almost all reinforcement learning problems can be defined using an MDP.

For understanding MDPs we need to use the concept of the **Markov reward process** (**MRP**). An MRP is a stochastic process which extends a Markov chain by adding a reward rate to each state. We can also define an additional variable to keep a track of the accumulated reward over time. Formally, an MRP is defined by (S, P, R, γ) where S is a finite state space, P is the state transition probability function, R is a reward function, γ and is the discount rate:

$$R_s = \mathbb{E}[R_{t+1} | S_t = S]$$

where $\mathbb{E}$ denotes the expectation. And the term R_s here denotes the expected reward at the state s.

In the case of MRPs, we can define the expected return when starting from a state s as:

$$v(s) = \mathbb{E}[G_t | S_t = s]$$

where G_t is the cumulative gain as we had defined in the previous section:

$$G_t = R_{t+1} + \gamma R_{t+1} + \gamma^2 R_{t+3} + \dots$$

$$G_t = \sum_{k=0}^{\infty} \gamma^k R_{t+k+1}$$

Now, for maximizing the cumulative reward, the agent will try to get the most expected sum of rewards from every state it goes into. To do that we need to find the optimal value function. We will see the algorithm for doing that in the next section.

Bellman equation

Using the Bellman equation, we decompose our value function into two separate parts, one representing the immediate reward and the other term representing the future rewards. From our previous definitions, the immediate reward is represented as R_{t+1} and the future rewards by $\gamma V(S_{t+1})$ where:

$$v(s) = \mathbb{E}[G_t | S_t = s]$$

Let's now unroll G_t and substitute G_{t+1} in it:

$$G_t = \mathbb{E}[R_{t+1}, \gamma R_{t+2} + \gamma^2 R_{t+3} + \ldots | S_t = s]$$
$$G_t = \mathbb{E}[R_{t+1}, \gamma (R_{t+2} + \gamma R_{t+3} + \ldots) | S_t = s]$$
$$G_t = \mathbb{E}[R_{t+1} + \gamma G_{t+1} | S_t = s]$$

Now, since we know that:

$$\mathbb{E}[aX + bY] = a\mathbb{E}[X] + b\mathbb{E}[Y]$$

Using this identity we have:

$$G_{t+1} = \mathbb{E}[R_{t+1} + \gamma v(S_{t+1}) | S_t = s]$$

And this gives us the Bellman equation for MRPs:

$$v(s) = \mathbb{E}[R_{t+1} + \gamma v(S_{t+1}) | S_t = s]$$

MDP

Now that we have a basic understanding of MRPs, we can move on to MDPs. An MDP is an MRP which also involved decisions. All the states in the environment are also Markov, hence the next state is only dependent on the current state. Formally, an MDP can be represented using (S, A, P, R, γ) where S is the state space, A is the action set, P is the state transition probability function, R is the reward function, and γ is the discount rate. The state transition probability function P and the reward function R are formally defined as:

$$P_{ss'}^a = \mathbb{P}[S_{t+1} = s' | S_t = s, A_t = a]$$
$$R_s^a = \mathbb{E}[R_{t+1} | S_t = s, A_t = a]$$

We can also formally define a policy π as:

$$\pi(a|s) = \mathbb{P}[A_t = a | S_t = s]$$

Since the states in the MDP are considered to be Markov, the MDP policies depend only on the current state, which means that the policies are stationary that $A_t \sim \pi(.|S_t) \; \forall t > 0$ is, . This means that whenever the agent falls into the same state, it will take the decision based on the same policy it had decided before. The decision function can be made stochastic so that the agent doesn't keep on taking the same decisions and hence is able to explore the environment.

Now, since we want to use the Bellman Equation in the case of MDP, we will recover an MRP from the MDPs. Given an MDP, $M = (S, A, P, R, \gamma)$ and a policy π the state sequence $S_1, S_2, ...$ is a Markov Process (S,P) on the policy π. The state and reward sequence S1, R1, S2, R2, ... is also an MRP given by (S, P, R, γ) where:

$$P_{ss'}^{\pi} = \sum_{a \in A} \pi(a|s) P_{ss'}^a$$

We can similarly formulate our reward function as:

$$R_s^{\pi} = \sum_{a \in A} \pi(a|s) R_s^a$$

And, since we know that the state-value function $V\pi(s)$ of an MDP is the expected return starting from state S and then following the policy π, the value function is given as:

$$v_{\pi}(s) = \mathbb{E}_{\pi}[G_t|S_t = s] = \mathbb{E}_{\pi}\left[\sum_{k=0}^{\infty} \gamma^k R_{t+k+1}\right]$$

Also, the action-value function can be given as:

$$q_{\pi}(s, a) = \mathbb{E}_{\pi}[G_t|S_t = s, A_t = a] = \mathbb{E}_{\pi}\left[\sum_{k=0}^{\infty} \gamma^k R_{t+k+1}|S_t = s, A_t = a\right]$$

Having these values, we can again derive the Bellman expectation equation in the case of MDPs. We again start by decomposing the state-value function into immediate reward and future rewards:

$$v_{\pi}(s) = \mathbb{E}_{\pi}[R_{t+1} + \gamma v_{\pi}(S_{t+1})|S_t = s]$$

And similar to the case of MRPs, the action-value function can also be decomposed as:

$$q_\pi(s, a) = \mathbb{E}_\pi[R_{t+1} + \gamma q_\pi(S_{t+1}, A_{t+1})|S_t = s, A_t = a]$$

And as we have multiple actions from each state S and the policy defines the probability distribution over the actions, we will need to average over it to get the Bellman expectation equation:

$$v_\pi(s) = \sum_{a \in A} \pi(a|s)q_\pi(s, a)$$

We can also average over all the possible action-values to know how good being in a given state S is:

$$q_\pi(s, a) = R_s^a + \gamma \sum_{s' \in S} P_{ss'}^a v_\pi(s')$$

Code example

In the following code example we implement a simple MDP:

```python
import numpy as np
import random


class MDP(object):
    """
    Defines a Markov Decision Process containing:
    - States, s
    - Actions, a
    - Rewards, r(s,a)
    - Transition Matrix, t(s,a,_s)

    Includes a set of abstract methods for extended class will
    need to implement.

    """

    def __init__(self, states=None, actions=None, rewards=None,
    transitions=None,
            discount=.99, tau=.01, epsilon=.01):
```

```
    """
    Parameters:
    -----------
    states: 1-D array
        The states of the environment

    actions: 1-D array
        The possible actions by the agent.

    rewards: 2-D array
        The rewards corresponding to each action at each state of the
environment.

    transitions: 2-D array
        The transition probabilities between the states of the environment.

    discount: float
        The discount rate for the reward.
    """
    self.s = np.array(states)
    self.a = np.array(actions)
    self.r = np.array(rewards)
    self.t = np.array(transitions)
    self.discount = discount
    self.tau = tau
    self.epsilon = epsilon

    # Value iteration will update this
    self.values = None
    self.policy = None

def getTransitionStatesAndProbs(self, state, action):
    """
    Returns the list of transition probabilities
    """
    return self.t[state][action][:]

def getReward(self, state):
    """
    Gets reward for transition from state->action->nextState.
    """
    return self.r[state]


def takeAction(self, state, action):
    """
    Take an action in an MDP, return the next state
```

Chooses according to probability distribution of state transitions, contingent on actions.

```python
        """
        return np.random.choice(self.s,
p=self.getTransitionStatesAndProbs(state, action))


    def valueIteration(self):
        """
        Performs value iteration to populate the values of all states in
        the MDP.

        """

        # Initialize V_0 to zero
        self.values = np.zeros(len(self.s))
        self.policy = np.zeros([len(self.s), len(self.a)])

        policy_switch = 0

        # Loop until convergence
        while True:

            # To be used for convergence check
            oldValues = np.copy(self.values)

            for i in range(len(self.s)-1):

                self.values[i] = self.r[i] + np.max(self.discount * \
                        np.dot(self.t[i][:][:], self.values))

            # Check Convergence
            if np.max(np.abs(self.values - oldValues)) <= self.epsilon:
                break


    def extractPolicy(self):
        """
        Extract policy from values after value iteration runs.
        """

        self.policy = np.zeros([len(self.s),len(self.a)])

        for i in range(len(self.s)-1):

            state_policy = np.zeros(len(self.a))
```

```
        state_policy = self.r[i] + self.discount* \
            np.dot(self.t[i][:][:], self.values)

        # Softmax the policy
        state_policy -= np.max(state_policy)
        state_policy = np.exp(state_policy / float(self.tau))
        state_policy /= state_policy.sum()

        self.policy[i] = state_policy



    def simulate(self, state):

        """

        Runs the solver for the MDP, conducts value iteration, extracts
    policy,
        then runs simulation of problem.

        NOTE: Be sure to run value iteration (solve values for states) and to
            extract some policy (fill in policy vector) before running
    simulation
        """
        # Run simulation using policy until terminal condition met
        while not self.isTerminal(state):

            # Determine which policy to use (non-deterministic)
            policy = self.policy[np.where(self.s == state)[0][0]]
            p_policy = self.policy[np.where(self.s == state)[0][0]] / \
                self.policy[np.where(self.s == state)[0][0]].sum()

            # Get the parameters to perform one move
            stateIndex = np.where(self.s == state)[0][0]
            policyChoice = np.random.choice(policy, p=p_policy)
            actionIndex =
    np.random.choice(np.array(np.where(self.policy[state][:] ==
    policyChoice)).ravel())

            # Take an action, move to next state
            nextState = self.takeAction(stateIndex, actionIndex)

            print "In state: {}, taking action: {}, moving to state: {}".format(
                state, self.a[actionIndex], nextState)

            # End game if terminal state reached
            state = int(nextState)
            if self.isTerminal(state):
```

```
        # print "Terminal state: {} has been reached. Simulation
over.".format(state)
        return state
```

Using this MDP, we can now code up a simple betting game:

```
class BettingGame(MDP):

    """

    Defines the Betting Game:

    Problem: A gambler has the chance to make bets on the outcome of
    a fair coin flip. If the coin is heads, the gambler wins as many
    dollars back as was staked on that particular flip - otherwise
    the money is lost. The game is won if the gambler obtains $100,
    and is lost if the gambler runs out of money (has 0$). This gambler
    did some research on MDPs and has decided to enlist them to assist
    in determination of how much money should be bet on each turn. Your
    task is to build that MDP!

    Params:

    pHead: Probability of coin flip landing on heads
    - Use .5 for fair coin, otherwise choose a bias [0,1]

    """

    def __init__(self, pHeads=.5, discount=.99, epsilon=.1, tau=.0001):

        MDP.__init__(self,discount=discount,tau=tau,epsilon=epsilon)
        self.pHeads = pHeads
        self.setBettingGame(pHeads)
        self.valueIteration()
        self.extractPolicy()

        # Edge case fix: Policy for $1
        self.policy[1][:] = 0
        self.policy[1][1] = 1.0

    def isTerminal(self, state):
        """
        Checks if MDP is in terminal state.
        """
        return True if state is 100 or state is 0 else False

    def setBettingGame(self, pHeads=.5):

        """
```

```
Initializes the MDP to the starting conditions for
the betting game.

Params:
pHeads = Probability that coin lands on head
- .5 for fair coin, otherwise choose bias

"""

# This is how much we're starting with
self.pHeads = pHeads

# Initialize all possible states
self.s = np.arange(102)

# Initialize possible actions
self.a = np.arange(101)

# Initialize rewards
self.r = np.zeros(101)
self.r[0] = -5
self.r[100] = 10

# Initialize transition matrix
temp = np.zeros([len(self.s),len(self.a),len(self.s)])

# List comprehension using tHelper to determine probabilities for each
index
self.t = [self.tHelper(i[0], i[1], i[2], self.pHeads) for i,x in
np.ndenumerate(temp)]
self.t = np.reshape(self.t, np.shape(temp))

for x in range(len(self.a)):

# Remember to add -1 to value it, and policy extract
# Send the end game states to the death state!
self.t[100][x] = np.zeros(len(self.s))
self.t[100][x][101] = 1.0
self.t[0][x] = np.zeros(len(self.s))
self.t[0][x][101] = 1.0


def tHelper(self, x, y, z, pHeads):

"""

Helper function to be used in a list comprehension to quickly
generate the transition matrix. Encodes the necessary conditions
to compute the necessary probabilities.
```

```
Params:
x,y,z indices
pHeads = probability coin lands on heads

"""

# If you bet no money, you will always have original amount
if x + y is z and y is 0:
return 1.0

# If you bet more money than you have, no chance of any outcome
elif y > x and x is not z:
return 0

# If you bet more money than you have, returns same state with 1.0 prob.
elif y > x and x is z:
return 1.0

# Chance you lose
elif x - y is z:
return 1.0 - pHeads

# Chance you win
elif x + y is z:
return pHeads

# Edge Case: Chance you win, and winnings go over 100
elif x + y > z and z is 100:
return pHeads


else:
return 0

return 0
```

Summary

In this chapter, we started with a short introduction to Reinforcement Learning. We talked about agents, rewards and our learning goals in reinforcement learning. In the next section, we introduced MRP which is one of the main concepts underlying MDP. Having an understanding of MRP we next introduce the concepts of MDP along with a code example.

Other Books You May Enjoy

If you enjoyed this book, you may be interested in these other books by Packt:

Machine Learning Algorithms - Second Edition
Giuseppe Bonaccorso

ISBN: 9781789347999

- Study feature selection and the feature engineering process
- Assess performance and error trade-offs for linear regression
- Build a data model and understand how it works by using different types of algorithm
- Learn to tune the parameters of Support Vector Machines (SVM)
- Explore the concept of natural language processing (NLP) and recommendation systems
- Create a machine learning architecture from scratch

Building Machine Learning Systems with Python - Third Edition
Luis Pedro Coelho, Willi Richert, Matthieu Brucher

ISBN: 9781788623223

- Build a classification system that can be applied to text, images, and sound
- Employ Amazon Web Services (AWS) to run analysis on the cloud
- Solve problems related to regression using scikit-learn and TensorFlow
- Recommend products to users based on their past purchases
- Understand different ways to apply deep neural networks on structured data
- Address recent developments in the field of computer vision and reinforcement learning

Leave a review - let other readers know what you think

Please share your thoughts on this book with others by leaving a review on the site that you bought it from. If you purchased the book from Amazon, please leave us an honest review on this book's Amazon page. This is vital so that other potential readers can see and use your unbiased opinion to make purchasing decisions, we can understand what our customers think about our products, and our authors can see your feedback on the title that they have worked with Packt to create. It will only take a few minutes of your time, but is valuable to other potential customers, our authors, and Packt. Thank you!

Index

forward-backward algorithm 64

G

gaussian distribution 74
grammatical tagging 113
greatest common divisor (GCD) 18

H

Hidden Markov Model (HMM)
  about 5, 33, 36, 49, 71, 99, 124
  Bayesian learning 94
  evaluation 43, 45
  extensions 45
  factorial HMMs 45
  observation sequence, generating 40
  parameterization 37, 38, 40
  Python packages, installing 42
  state inference 49, 52
  tree-structured HMM 46
  used, for predicting prices 104, 108
  using, for stock price prediction 99
history of the agent 148
hitting time 22
homogenous model 39

I

independent and identically distributed (IID) 72, 146
inference 49
inference algorithms 49

L

Linux
  Python, installing 9

M

Markov chains
  about 9, 10, 12
  distributions, limiting 24
  ergodicity 24
  parameterization 12, 14
  periodicity 18, 19
  properties 15
  recurrence 20

reducibility 15, 17
steady-state analysis 24
transience 20
Markov Decision Process (MDP) 145
Markov models
  about 33
  state space models 34, 36
Markov process 7
Markov property 7
Markov reward process (MRP)
  about 150
  Bellman equation 150
  MDP 151, 153
maximum a posteriori (MAP) 84, 93
maximum likelihood estimation (MLE)
  about 71
  code 86, 89
  coin, tossing 72, 74
  for HMMs 77
  for normal distributions 74, 76, 77
  supervised learning 78
  unsupervised learning 81
MDP 151, 153
mean recurrence time 22
memoization 52
memoryless systems 7
Miniconda
  URL 8
most frequent class tagger (MFC Tagger) 119

N

null recurrent 22

O

observation sequence
  generating 40
overfitting 91

P

packages
  installing 8
part-of-speech tagging (POS tagging)
  about 113
  code 114
  data, exploring 117

CPSIA information can be obtained
at www.ICGtesting.com
Printed in the USA
FSHW011324090720
71568FS